UNDERSTANDING EUROPEAN UNION LAW

European Union law is now a core subject for both the Bar Council and the Law Society, and it is vital that all law students equip themselves with a sound understanding of the EU legal system.

This fully revised third edition looks at the main themes of EU law in a logical, progressive manner, giving the reader an understanding of EU law, concentrating on how, and especially why, the law has developed as it has. In addition, a number of issues presently facing the EU are also considered, such as enlargement and the prospect of a comprehensive written constitution. C

- Introduction
- The Creation of a European Union
- Who Runs Europe?
- Community Law

- The Relationship Between Community Law and the Member States
- Enforcing Community Law
- Free Movement of Goods
- Free Movement of Persons and Services
- Competition Law
- Revision and Examinations

Incorporating summaries, comprehensive and updated tables of cases and legislation, a list of abbreviations, a glossary of terms and important tips on how to approach examination questions, this student-friendly text is broad in scope and highly accessible. *Understanding European Union Law* is both an introduction for students new to EU law and an essential addition to revision for the more accomplished. It is also essential reading for students on business studies courses.

The ultimate objective of this book is to show that understanding EU law can be an enjoyable and rewarding experience!

Karen Davies, LLB, LLM, is a Lecturer in Law at the University of Wales, Swansea and is also an Associate Lecturer with the Open University.

UNDERSTANDING EUROPEAN UNION LAW

Third edition first published 2007
by Routledge-Cavendish
2 Park Square, Milton Park, Abingdon, Oxon OX14 4RN

Simultaneously published in the USA and Canada
by Routledge-Cavendish
270 Madison Ave, New York, NY 10016

Reprinted 2007 (twice), 2008

Routledge-Cavendish is an imprint of the Taylor & Francis Group, an informa business

© 2001, 2003, 2007 Karen Davies

Previous editions published by Cavendish Publishing Ltd
First edition 2001
Second edition 2003

Typeset in Palatino by
Newgen Imaging Systems (P) Ltd, Chennai, India
Printed and bound in Great Britain by
MPG Books Ltd, Bodmin, Cornwall

British Library Cataloguing in Publication Data
A catalogue record for this book is available
from the British Library

Library of Congress Cataloging in Publication Data
Davies, Karen, LLB
    Understanding European Union law / Karen Davies. – 3rd ed.
      p. cm.
    Rev. ed. of: Understanding EU law. 2nd ed. 2003.
    Includes bibliographical references and index.
      1. Law–European Union countries. I. Davies, Karen, LLB.
    Understanding EU law. II. Title. III. Title: Understanding EU law.

KJE949.D38 2007
341.242'2–dc22   2006022565

ISBN10: 0–415–41977–8 (pbk)
ISBN13: 978–0–415–41977–2 (pbk)

Contents

Table of Cases

Table of Legislation

Glossary

Acquis communautaire	The body of objectives, substantive rules, policies, laws, rights, remedies and case law fundamental to the development of the Community legal order.
Advocates General	Assistants to the European Court of Justice, having the same status as judges.
Assembly	Original name given to the European Parliament.
Assent procedure	The legislative procedure whereby the Council must obtain the Parliament's agreement before certain important decisions may be taken. Introduced by the SEA.
Budget	The Union's revenue and expenditure. The Commission is responsible for submitting a draft budget annually to the Council, which shares budgetary authority with the Parliament.
Charges having equivalent effect	Charges having an equivalent effect to customs duties and, as such, prohibited by Community law.
Charter of Fundamental Rights (of the European Union)	Charter which summarises the common values of the Member States of the European Union.
Citizenship	Citizenship of the Union is dependent on holding nationality of one of the Member States (Art 17 of the EC Treaty).
Co-decision procedure	The legislative procedure whereby the European Parliament is given the power to adopt acts jointly with the Council. Introduced by the TEU (Art 251 of the EC Treaty).

Comitology	The process by which the Commission is assisted by committees in the implementation of legislation.
Committee of the Regions	The European Union's youngest institution whose birth reflects Member States' strong desire not only to respect regional and local identities and prerogatives, but also to involve them in the development and implementation of EU policies.
Common customs tariff	The common customs duty encircling the Community, charged at the same level no matter where a product is cleared for customs (Arts 23–26 of the EC Treaty).
Common policies	Includes common policies on agriculture, commerce and transport, established to ensure common principles and aims throughout the Community.
Community competence	The Community is based on the principle of limited powers which are specifically attributed to it by the Treaties. Before the Community may take action, it must ensure that it has been provided with the authority to do so.
Community law	The rules of the Community legal order including primary and secondary legislation, general principles of law and case law of the European Court of Justice. Also known as the acquis.
Competencies	Power and responsibilities of the EU, its Institutions and national authorities.
Competition rules	Community rules intended to ensure that competition in the Community is not distorted.
Conciliation Committee	Conciliation Committees may be set up under the co-decision (legislative) procedure with the aim of reaching agreement between the Council and the Parliament in relation to a legislative proposal (Art 251 of the EC Treaty).
Consultation procedure	A legislative procedure under which the Council is bound to consult with the European Parliament and take its views into account.

Consumer protection	Inserted by the TEU, it is intended to promote consumer health, safety, economic and legal interest, and their right to information (Art 153 of the EC Treaty).
Convergence criteria	Criteria that must be attained by those Member States wishing to join the European Single Currency.
Co-operation procedure	A legislative procedure, introduced by the SEA, giving the Parliament greater influence in the creation of Community legislation.
COREPER	Name commonly given to the Committee of Permanent Representatives who carry out tasks on behalf of the Council. They also provide a forum in which legislation can be discussed and agreed.
Council of the European Union	More usually known as the Council of Ministers, it has no equivalent anywhere in the world. It is here that the Member States legislate for the Union, set its political objectives, co-ordinate their national policies and resolve differences between themselves and with other institutions.
Court of Auditors	The taxpayers' representative, responsible for checking that the European Union spends its money according to its budgetary rules and regulations and for the purposes for which it is intended.
Court of First Instance	Established by the SEA, the Court has taken over some of the workload of the ECJ, allowing that Court to concentrate on its fundamental task of ensuring the uniform interpretation of Community law.
Court of Justice	Provides the judicial safeguards necessary to ensure that the law is observed in the interpretation and application of the Treaties and, generally, in all of the activities of the Union. (Normally referred to as the 'Court' with a capital C.)
Customs Union	An area where barriers to trade have been eliminated, as exists between the Member States (Arts 23–27 of the EC Treaty).

Decision making	The processes by which decisions are taken or legislative acts are created within the Community/Union.
Decisions	Community legislative acts which are binding upon those to whom they are addressed (Art 249 of the EC Treaty).
Deepening	The process of increased integration between the Member States.
Democratic deficit	Criticism levied at the Community in relation to its perceived remoteness from the ordinary citizen, particularly in relation to the creation of legislation.
Direct applicability	A directly applicable provision of European law is one which takes effect within the Member States without the need for incorporation or implementation by national authorities.
Direct effect	A doctrine established by the European Court of Justice providing that Community law may provide rights and obligations to individuals, enforceable in national courts.
Direct elections	Democratic elections held to elect the Members of the European Parliament (MEPs) (Art 190 of the EC Treaty).
Directives	Legislative acts that oblige Member States to implement the aims contained within the directive by a stipulated date.
Distinctly applicable measure (DAM)	Term used to describe restrictive measures, enacted by Member States, which discriminate between nationally produced goods and those originating in other States.
Dualist State	A State, such as the United Kingdom, in which international law and national law are considered distinct and separate from one another.
Economic and Monetary Union	The process whereby the economic and monetary policies of the Member States are harmonised, culminating in the introduction of a single currency.

Economic and Social Committee	In accordance with the Treaties, the Committee advises the Commission, the Council and the European Parliament. The opinions which it delivers (either in response to a referral or on its own initiative) are drawn up by representatives of the various categories of economic and social activity in the European Union.
Effet utile	A principle of law developed by the European Court of Justice to ensure effective enforcement of Community rules within the Member States.
Enlargement	*See* Widening.
Euratom	European Community created in 1957 in order to integrate the nuclear industries of the Member States, promoting safety, research, etc.
Euro	European unit of currency.
European Central Bank	The decision making body in relation to European Monetary Union, responsible for implementing the monetary policy of the Union.
European Coal and Steel Community	European Community created in 1951 in order to integrate the coal and steel industries of the Member States.
European Commission	A Community institution which has three distinct functions: initiator of proposals for legislation, guardian of the Treaties and the manager and executor of Union policies and of international trade relations.
European Community (EC)	Community created in 1957 by the Treaty of Rome. Once named the European Economic Community (renamed by the TEU) in order to integrate the economies of the Member States (see Art 2 of the EC Treaty and the Preamble to the EC Treaty).
European Communities	Pillar I of the European Union, comprising the EC, ECSC and Euratom.
European Communities Act	Enacted in the UK in 1972 in order to incorporate the law of the European Community into the law of the United Kingdom.

European Convention on Human Rights	Signed under the aegis of the Council of Europe. While the Community/Union has not acceded to the Convention, respect for fundamental human rights has been formalised by the Treaty of Amsterdam.
European Council	The name given to the meetings of the Heads of State of the Member States. Over the last two decades, its summit meetings have played a crucial role in the development of the EU.
European Investment Bank	The European Union's financing institution; it provides loans for capital investment, promoting the Union's balanced economic development and integration.
European Parliament	The directly elected democratic expression of the political will of the peoples of the European Union; the largest multinational Parliament in the world.
Federalism	System of government where competencies are shared amongst different levels of government.
General principles	A body of unwritten principles supplementing Community legislation and developed by the ECJ from the threads found in the Treaties, the laws of the Member States and international law.
Harmonisation	The process of approximation laws throughout the Member States in order to ensure the establishment and effective functioning of the internal market.
High Authority	The original name for what has become the European Commission.
Indirect effect	Doctrine developed by the ECJ requiring national courts to interpret national legislation in the light of European directives.
Indistinctly applicable measure (IDAM)	Restrictive measures enacted by Member States, which apply equally to domestically produced goods and those produced in other States.
Institutions	Five institutions that have been afforded powers by the Treaties in order to ensure aims set out in the EC Treaty are realised (Art 7).

Intergovernmental conference	Conferences of the Heads of State of the Member States held with the specific purpose of amending the primary legislation of the EC/EU.
Intergovernmentalism	A theory of integration under which the Member States take decisions by co-operation and consensus.
Internal market	The creation of an internal market is the first of three stages in the creation of an European Union, the others being monetary and political union. It involves uniting the markets of the Member States into a single economic area without internal frontiers.
Judicial review	Term commonly used to describe the various actions available to the ECJ in order to review the legality of acts of the institutions.
Locus Standi	The right to be heard in court or other proceeding.
Luxembourg Accords/ Compromise	Agreement reached, in 1966, following the French refusal to accept majority voting in the Council. It allowed Member States to request that decisions be reached by unanimity, rather than majority, when an issue was considered to be of major national interest.
Measures having equivalent effect	Measures having an equivalent effect to quantitative restrictions on trade and held to include State measures which discriminate against imports (DAMs) and those which treat imports and domestic goods alike (IDAMs).
Monist State	A State in which international law is incorporated into the national legal system as soon as it is ratified.
Multi-speed Europe	A term used to describe the system whereby a group of Member States is willing to make an advance in the assumption that other States will follow later. Also known as 'variable geometry'.
Official Journal	A publication of the European Community in which regulations and directives must be published, together with other legislative and non-binding acts.

Ombudsman	Every citizen of each Member State is both a national and a European citizen. One of the rights of all European citizens is to apply to the European Ombudsman if they are victims of an act of 'maladministration' by the institutions or bodies.
Pillars of the European Union	The EU is said to be made up of three pillars of which the European Communities comprise the first pillar, common foreign and security policy the second, whilst police and judicial co-operation in criminal matters forms the third.
Preliminary reference	A term describing the procedure by which national courts may request a ruling from the ECJ on the interpretation of primary and secondary Community legislation and on the validity of secondary legislation (Art 234 of the EC Treaty).
Proportionality	Measures which are appropriate and necessary to achieve an object.
Purposive method of interpretation	Method of legislative interpretation favoured by the ECJ in which the provision of Community law must be put into context and interpreted in the light of the law as a whole. Also alluded to as the teleological or contextual method.
Qualified majority voting	A procedure for reaching agreement in Council by which each Member Stateís votes are weighted to reflect the population of that State (Art 205 of the EC Treaty).
Quantitative restriction	Non-pecuniary restrictions placed on goods by virtue of their crossing a frontier, for example, quotas and total bans.
Regulations	Legislative acts of the institutions of the Community which take effect in all Member States without the need for enacting measures on the part of those States.
Schengen Agreement	An agreement between a number of Member States to abolish checks at common borders in order to achieve free movement of persons.

Single European Act	Amending Treaty signed in 1986 by the Member States. Its main aim was to speed up integration in the Community and it also laid down provisions relating to political co-operation.
Soft law	Rules which have no binding force, but which may nevertheless have practical effects.
Subsidiarity	A principle ensuring that decisions are taken as closely as possible to the citizen in areas which are not in the exclusive competence of the Community/Union.
Supranationalism	A theory of integration involving power moving from the Member States to the institutions.
Supremacy	A doctrine developed by the ECJ, providing that, where Community law and national law conflict, Community law will take precedence.
Transparency	A term used by the institutions to denote openness in their workings. It includes a commitment to access to information (Art 255 of the EC Treaty).
Treaty of Amsterdam	An amending treaty introduced in 1999. Its main aims are to place the interests of workers and citizens at the heart of the Union, to remove existing barriers to free movement while improving security, give the Union a greater voice on the world stage and ensure that the institutions are as effective and efficient as possible in preparation for enlargement.
Treaty of Nice	Signed in 2000, came into effect in February 2003, an amending Treaty with the aim of facilitating the enlargement of the EU.
Treaty on European Union	Signed in 1992, the Treaty not only amended the EC Treaty, but also created the European Union of which the European Communities form a part.
Twin pillars	The 'twin pillars' of direct effect and supremacy of EC law – not to be confused with the three pillars of the EU.

Variable geometry	*See* Multi-speed Europe.
Widening	A term used to describe the enlargement of the European Community/Union. At present, a number of former eastern bloc countries are attempting to attain the necessary criteria, together with Malta, Cyprus and Turkey.

Abbreviations

AG	Advocate General
Art	Article
CCT	common customs tariff
CFI	Court of First Instance
CHEE	charge having equivalent effect
CMLR	Common Market Law Review
CoA	Court of Auditors
CoR	Committee of Regions
COREPER	Committee of Permanent Representatives
CU	Customs Union
DAM	distinctly applicable measure
DG	directorate-general
EC	European Community/Treaty establishing the European Community
ECB	European Central Bank
ECHR	European Convention for the Protection of Human Rights and Fundamental Freedoms/ European Court of Human Rights
ECJ	European Court of Justice
ECOSOC	Economic and Social Committee
ECR	European Court Reports
ECSC	European Coal and Steel Community
EEC	European Economic Community
EIB	European Investment Bank

EMU	European Monetary Union
EP	European Parliament
ESCB	European System of Central Banks
ET	employment tribunal
EU	European Union
Euratom	European Atomic Energy Community
IDAM	indistinctly applicable measure
IGC	intergovernmental conference
IPR	intellectual property right
MEP	Member of the European Parliament
MHEE	measure having equivalent effect
NATO	North Atlantic Treaty Organisation
OEEC	Organisation for Economic Co-operation
OJ	Official Journal
QMV	qualified majority voting
QR	Quantitative Restrictions
RGM	relevant geographical market
RPM	relevant product market
SEA	Single European Act 1986
TEU	Treaty on European Union 1992
ToA	Treaty of Amsterdam 1997
ToN	Treaty of Nice 2000

1 Introduction

I. THE SIGNIFICANCE OF EUROPEAN LAW

The UK's membership of the European Community (EC), which itself is now part of the broader European Union (EU), means that European law has become an integral source of UK law. Knowledge and understanding of the law of the Community is therefore indispensable to all lawyers in the United Kingdom.

II. THE AIMS OF THIS BOOK

In recognition of the importance of European law, it is vital that law students have a solid grounding in its principles. Many students appear, however, to find the study of Community law rather alarming, which is perhaps understandable given the differences of approach and language that exist between the Community's legal system and that of the United Kingdom.

Students of European law should, however, take heart. The main body of Community law goes back little more than 50 years and has generally developed with a set of specific aims in mind, which means that it is possible to approach it in a logical, incremental manner. That is not to say that the scope of EC law is narrow. Indeed, it is not and it would be impossible to cover all that it encompasses, in any degree of depth, in a single volume.

In recognition of the breadth of Community law, the content of most European law courses is necessarily limited to the principal constitutional and institutional areas of the Community legal order, together with selected areas of substantive law.

Despite this approach, there are still huge areas of law to cover and although there are a number of excellent textbooks providing detailed accounts of the law, such texts can be intimidating or overpowering and, consequently, rather daunting to the new student.

While this book aims to provide an account of the same constitutional and institutional principles together with important areas of substantive law, albeit in a less circuitous manner than many texts, a different approach has been taken. At the beginning of each topic, before the legal principles are examined, each area of law is put into context, thus allowing an understanding of relevant issues to be developed.

In addition, at the end of most sections, knowledge and understanding are consolidated by the provision of diagrams and/or flowcharts that clearly highlight the main points at issue.

This approach is intended to encourage an understanding of European law as a whole, allowing students to develop a 'feel' for the subject and, ultimately, resulting in far less rote learning being necessary just before examinations!

III. HOW TO STUDY EU LAW

Your approach to studying European law can undoubtedly make all the difference to your enjoyment of the course and also to the end result. The subject of the UK's membership of the EU is one of keen debate in the media and it is almost impossible not to have formed some sort of opinion as to whether Britain should be 'in' or 'out'! Certain UK newspapers appear to thrive on discussion as to whether Europe should dictate the shape of the bananas we eat or whether hedgehog flavoured crisps should be banned and it is often difficult to arrive at the study of European law with an open mind. However, this is an essential prerequisite to successful study!

During your course you will be expected to attend lectures and tutorials. Do not underestimate the importance of these. We all learn in various ways, not only through what we read, but also by listening, seeing and doing. Reading various texts, periodicals and so on is essential, but attending lectures can focus the mind, provide an introduction to a topic, shed light on areas of confusion and afford an alternative point of view!

Similarly, tutorial attendance has numerous advantages (and attendance is often mandatory, if you wish to stay on the course!). It allows various topics or points to be focused upon, it provides opportunity for discussion, it allows for clarification and is also likely to provide invaluable practice in answering exam-type questions, both essay and problem solving. Be sure not to miss out on these opportunities.

IV. FINDING OUT ABOUT EUROPEAN LAW

1. Resources

There is a wealth of sources of information on the EU and Community law. Those enrolled on a structured course will normally be provided with at least an outline reading list of appropriate textbooks and useful legal journals.

Make sure you have an up to date copy of EC legislation at the start of your course. If used regularly, you will find it invaluable. The EC Treaty and secondary legislation are, by and large, very readable and you should *always* read the various Treaty articles and secondary legislation as you study them.

In addition to these traditional sources of legal information, Internet access has opened up a huge source of materials. The number of websites containing information on Community law appears to grow daily and it is a virtually impossible task to provide a comprehensive list. Do, however, take care only to consult those sites which are recognised legal databases. The EU also has its own site, which is a good place to begin as it also provides a number of links to other relevant sites. The address of this site is http://europa.eu.int.

Furthermore, the Community institutions produce a wealth of literature (including CD-ROMs) on various aspects of the EC and EU, much of which is free. A list of such publications, together with details of how to order, can be found on the Europa website.

V. BEGINNING YOUR STUDIES

1. Coping with jargon

Law students often remark that, when they embark on a course of study of a particular branch of law, not only do they have to take on board new legal principles, statutes, case law and so onbut they also have to cope with legal jargon that is particular to that area of law. This is certainly true of

European law and students new to the subject may find themselves confused by terminology.

In order to overcome this problem (which can have serious consequences, as students who fail to break through the jargon may never fully understand the law beyond), this book provides a Glossary of commonly used terms. It is advisable to glance through this at the beginning of any course of study and it should be regularly referred to throughout.

2. EC or EU?

One important piece of terminology that needs to be understood from the outset is the difference between the EC and the EU. The terms are often used interchangeably, yet can mean very different things. As you will soon discover, the EC, once known as the European Economic Community, was created under the Treaty of Rome in 1957. The EU was, on the other hand, created by the Treaty on European Union in 1992. The confusion arises because the EU is a complex structure made up of a number of parts, one of which is the EC. The EC is therefore part of the EU, but not the same as it! This should become clearer once Chapter 2 has been read and digested.

3. Dealing with case names

In addition to the often oblique terminology which has been adopted by European lawyers, students of EC law often find the names of the decisions of the European Court of Justice to be a nightmare!

When it is considered that the EU is comprised of 25 States and has almost as many official languages, it is understandable that case names should occasionally prove difficult to pronounce and spell. Few lawyers would pretend that Case 109/88, *Handels-OG Kontorfunktionaernesforbund v Dansk Arbeejdsgiverforening*, flows easily off either the tongue or the pen. Despair may be avoided, however, once you understand that many EC law cases have nicknames that are often acceptable for use in examinations (but do check with your tutor). For example, the commonly used and accepted nickname for the above case is *Danfoss* which, I am sure you will agree, is quite manageable!

4. Making sure you know 'which way you are going'

Life can be made far easier if we know which direction we are going in. If we are unsure, then life can be very confusing. The same can be said of studying European law. It is not sufficient to know that you are going to study EC law. In order to make studying as painless as possible, and even enjoyable, you need to have some knowledge of precisely what areas of law you are going to study and why and also in what order various topics are to be considered.

If you are provided with a course guide or timetable, such information is often contained within it. Generally, undergraduate EC law courses follow the following scheme, which should be roughly that of this book.

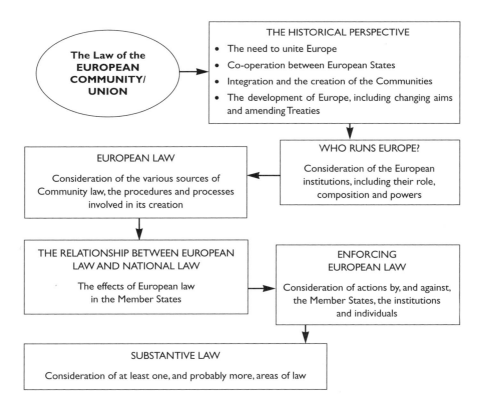

VI. CONCLUSIONS

Hopefully, this book will not be seen as just another simplified or insubstantial text but rather as an introduction to European law, which ensures that all who access it provide themselves with firm foundations on which to build greater and deeper knowledge. No strong, high or long-lasting wall was ever built without a sound foundation being put in place first!

Remember that this book does not profess to contain all you will need to know about the law of the European Community but, hopefully, it will provide the desire and the tools to study further. Finally, if there is something you do not understand, please do not let it blight your studies – if you do not know, find a man (or woman) who does, and ASK! Most tutors worth their salt will be only too pleased to help.

2 The Creation of a European Union

I. WHY WERE THE EUROPEAN COMMUNITIES CREATED?

The best way to understand European law is to start at the beginning, which inevitably involves some consideration of why the Community exists at all. The idea of a united Europe is certainly not a new one and a variety of leaders have, over the centuries, attempted to achieve European integration. In more modern times, it is possible to highlight the end of the Second World War in 1945 as the catalyst which set in motion events that have led to the creation of a European Union.

The economies of the European States had been devastated by war and the peoples of Europe were anxious to build a peaceful and more stable future for themselves. The United States saw a union between the European States as a means of countering a perceived communist threat from the eastern bloc countries and, consequently, provided financial aid, under what became known as the Marshall Plan. In order to administer this programme of aid, the Organisation for Economic Co-operation was set up in 1948, inevitably involving co-operation between recipient States. Other organisations such as the North Atlantic Treaty Organisation (NATO), whose aims primarily related to defence, were also created and can be seen as early forms of modern co-operation in Europe.

1. The Council of Europe

Further co-operation between European governments led, in 1947, to the creation of the Council of Europe, an intergovernmental organisation (use the Glossary!) which adopted the European Convention on Human Rights and established the European Court of Human Rights. *It needs to be emphasised from the outset, however, that this organisation is totally separate from that which has become known as the European Community/Union.* While undoubtedly performing valuable tasks, particularly in the area of human rights, the Council of Europe fell short of what many felt was needed in order to stabilise inter-State relationships and ensure economic regeneration.

2. The First European Community: The European Coal and Steel Community (ECSC)

A plan based on economic co-operation in Europe was proposed by Jean Monnet and taken up by Robert Schuman, the then French Foreign Minister. This embryonic scheme involved the integration of the French and German coal and steel industries as a means of stabilising the relationship between the two countries. The plan allowed two 'war-making' industries to be monitored, ensuring that the capacity of the parties to secretly rearm was reduced. However, as the idea also included ensuring security on a wider European scale, an invitation to participate was proffered to other countries and the ECSC was finally created by the signing of the Treaty of Paris in 1951. This new Community had an initial membership of six, namely France, Germany, Italy, Belgium, Luxembourg and the Netherlands (the then British Prime Minister, Sir Anthony Eden, had declared that the United Kingdom had no need to join, as it was well able to 'stand on its own two feet' – a reference to the UK's links with both the Commonwealth and the United States).

The creation of the ECSC was particularly significant, as it moved away from the more traditional intergovernmental system of co-operation between participating States. Four independent institutions were created to run the Community and the power to control the coal and steel industries was moved from the participating States to these institutions, which comprised a High Authority, an Assembly, a Council and a Court of Justice (the ECJ). The new Community consequently had a decidedly supranational, rather than intergovernmental, flavour. It is interesting to note that, although 50 years have gone by since this transfer of 'sovereign powers' first took place, as we shall see later, the extent of this transfer of authority still remains a matter of debate and contention within the EU.

While the immediate focus of the ECSC was undoubtedly economic, that is, the creation of a common market in coal and steel, with common policies and the removal of all barriers to trade in those commodities, it should not be forgotten that the contracting States saw economic co-operation as a means to an end. Ensuring that the longer term aims of peace and European unity were achieved was still the focus, if not the immediate emphasis, of the Community. This can be evidenced by reference to the Preamble to the Treaty of Paris, which provides that the establishment of an economic community is a 'basis for a broader and deeper community among peoples long divided by bloody conflicts; and to lay the foundations for institutions which will give direction to a destiny henceforward shared'.

It should be noted that the Treaty of Paris expired in July 2002. All ECSC funds have been transferred to the EC, to be used for research in sectors relating to the coal and steel industries.

3. The European Atomic Energy Community (Euratom)

Following the creation of the ECSC, further attempts at integration between the contracting States were made, with plans being drawn up for a European Defence Community and European Political Community, involving the creation of a European army and a common European foreign policy. Agreement could not, however, be reached on these matters and it was not until 1956 that a way forward towards further integration was found. A report was published by an intergovernmental committee chaired by Paul-Henri Spaak, the then Belgian Foreign Minister, detailing plans for a further two communities, the European Atomic Energy Community (Euratom) and the European Economic Community (EEC).

The Euratom Treaty was signed in Rome in 1957 by the same six countries that had previously joined together to form the ECSC. The object of this new Community can be summarised as the furtherance of atomic energy for peaceful purposes, together with a commitment to uniform safety standards. Once more, as for the ECSC, the control of each Member State's atomic industries was passed to four autonomous institutions, with the Assembly and the ECJ being common to both Communities.

4. The European Economic Community (EEC)

Like Euratom, the EEC was born as a result of the Spaak Report and the Treaty establishing the EEC was signed in Rome by the same six Member States, on the same day as the Euratom Treaty. A further similarity lies in the fact that the new Community was to be administered by four independent institutions upon whom the Member States had delegated the right of independent action in certain specified areas. (Once more, the ECJ and the Assembly were shared between the Communities.)

Both the ECSC and Euratom were, however, limited in their scope, being functionalist in that they had as their aims the creation of a common market in coal and steel and in atomic energy, respectively. The EEC was significantly broader in its approach, in that it was created with the task of working towards integration of all aspects of the economies of its Member States, rather than integration of specific industries.

While the vehicle for integration was once more economic, the Preamble to the EEC Treaty again suggested that longer term goals were wider, including a determination to 'lay the foundations of an ever closer union among the peoples of Europe'. This was very much in line with Monnet and Schuman's view that integration of the Member States' economies would spill over into other areas, namely political and social.

II. THE DEVELOPMENT OF THE EUROPEAN COMMUNITIES

The term 'European Communities' is used to denote all three Communities, that is, the ECSC, Euratom and the EEC. This should not be confused with the European Community (EC), which is the new name for the EEC, as introduced by the Treaty on European Union (which is discussed below). The Communities have not stood still since their inception and, in order to fully understand their present position, the major milestones in their development need to be considered.

1. The Merger Treaty 1965

The Merger Treaty, which came into effect in 1967, was the first amendment to the Treaties of Paris and Rome. Its main purpose was to merge the institutions of all three Communities, creating a common Council of Ministers and a common Commission (formerly known as the High Authority). The remaining two institutions, the European Parliament (EP) (formerly the Assembly) and the ECJ, already served all three Communities.

2. The Single European Act 1986

The Single European Act (SEA), which came into effect in 1987, is considered to be the first substantial revision of the Treaties. While considerable early success had been enjoyed, progress with regards to further integration had slowed to near-stagnation. This virtual standstill was blamed on a number of factors, both external and internal, including world recession and difficulties relating to decision making within the EEC, and the SEA can be viewed as a response to such problems.

The SEA contains a number of important provisions, both amending the original treaties and also laying down provisions for political co-operation between the Member States.

First, the new Treaty formalised European political co-operation by recognising the European Council and providing for twice-yearly meetings. (A note of warning: take care not to confuse the European Council with the Council of Ministers or the Council of the European Union as it is now known. The European Council is a separate organisation created in 1974, with a membership composed of the Heads of State or Government of the Member States, foreign ministers and the Commission President.)

The SEA also amended the existing Treaties in an attempt to ensure increased efficiency and democracy within the institutional framework. A Court of First Instance (CFI) was created to assist the overworked ECJ. In addition, a new legislative procedure, known as 'co-operation', was introduced which provided the EP with increased influence in the legislative process. The Parliament was also given the right of veto over the accession of new Member States. (Changes to the Parliament's functions were a response to calls for an enhanced role following the introduction of direct elections for Members of the European Parliament (MEPs) by citizens of the Member States. The first elections took place in 1979 and were significant, in that the Parliament became the first – and only – Community institution to receive a direct, democratic mandate.)

In an attempt to revitalise progress towards economic integration, the SEA also introduced an 'Internal Market' to be attained by a set date: 31 December 1992. Also known as the 'single market', the Internal Market was intended to take the Community beyond being merely a customs union (i.e. an area without internal barriers to trade) to a Community with complete totality of economic activity.

It was realised that the creation of a single market would require substantial legislative activity by the institutions and, with this in mind, the SEA introduced a change to voting procedures in the Council. The use of qualified majority voting (whereby each Council Minister's vote is

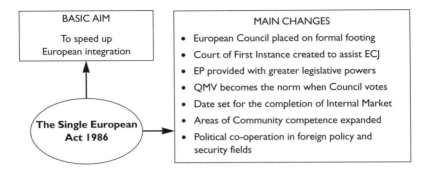

'weighted', reflecting the population of the Member State) was significantly increased and, with the corresponding move away from the need for unanimity, the legislative process was effectively speeded up. (It is far easier and quicker to ensure majority agreement to a legislative proposal than to achieve unanimity.)

The SEA also extended the existing substantive areas of Community competence, formally recognising co-operation in economic and monetary union, social policy, economic and social cohesion (i.e. reducing disparity between the various regions within the Community), research and technological development and action on protection of the environment.

Finally, the treaty referred to political co-operation, albeit outside formal Community structures. It provided for the inclusion of the Commission and EP within the process and also for the development of co-operation in foreign policy and security fields (thus creating the forerunner of the three pillared EU, which is discussed below).

While the SEA has not been without its critics, who decried it as vague and ambiguous, it undoubtedly gave renewed momentum to plans for the economic integration of Europe and also laid important foundations for social and political integration. Institutional changes introduced by the Act supported the supranational nature of the Communities by increasing the influence of both the Parliament and the Commission while, at the same time, qualified majority voting (QMV) was recognised as the norm in Council, decreasing the influence of individual Member States.

3. The Treaty on European Union 1992

The Treaty on European Union (TEU), also commonly known as the Maastricht Treaty after the Netherlands town where it was signed, was created with two broad aims in mind: first, to sustain the momentum created by the SEA and, second, the creation of a new organisation, albeit founded on the original Communities, to be known as the European Union (EU). The Treaty itself can be divided into two distinct parts: that which amends the original Treaties and that which created the EU.

i. Changes to the original treaties

Significantly, the TEU renamed the EEC the EC, with the Treaty creating the EEC also being renamed the EC Treaty. It can be argued that the removal of the term 'economic' from the Community's title was intended to indicate that, with the process of economic integration nearing completion, the EC could now begin to concentrate on moving towards further integration in social and political areas.

The TEU also broadened the aims of the Community to include such objectives as monetary union and social and environmental protection. In addition, the new Treaty provided for institutional and legislative changes, together with a timetable for the introduction of European Monetary Union (EMU). New areas of Community competence were introduced, while others were expanded. While the main changes are highlighted immediately below, they will be further discussed, as appropriate, in later chapters.

The EP's involvement in the legislative process was once more increased by extended use of the co-operation procedure (introduced by the SEA) and the introduction of a new procedure known as co-decision, which effectively allows the Parliament to 'veto' legislative proposals. In addition, the Parliament was given a right of initiative with regard to legislation, once a monopoly enjoyed by the Commission. The Parliament was also afforded the power to appoint a European Ombudsman to investigate complaints relating to alleged maladministration on the part of the Community institutions and their staff.

Other changes involving the institutions included formally recognising the Court of Auditors (CoA) as a Community institution and the creation of a European Central Bank (ECB).

The TEU introduced the concept of European citizenship, which is provided to nationals of the Member States. With regard to issues relating to economic and monetary policy, the path towards EMU was further elaborated upon and a timetable set for its various stages, climaxing with the adoption of a single currency. A new timetable for the free movement of capital was also introduced.

ii. Creation of the EU

The TEU created a 'three pillared' structure, comprising the following:

- Pillar I, comprising of the ECSC, Euratom and the EC;

- Pillar II, providing for the development of policies relating largely to the Member States and their relationship with the rest of the world;

- Pillar III, providing for inter-State co-operation on policies including asylum, external border controls, immigration and international fraud together with judicial co-operation on civil and criminal matters, and police co-operation relating to terrorism and drugs.

(Note that the content of these pillars has now changed, as discussed below.)

In contrast with the EC, the EU does not have separate legal personality and, with regard to Pillars II and III, there was no transfer of sovereign powers from the Member States. Instead, progress under Pillars II and III relied on intergovernmental co-operation and consensus amongst the Member States. This did not mean, however, that there was to be no institutional involvement. While the European Council took the major political decisions of the EU, the Council of Ministers, which represents the Member States, was provided with a central decision-making role. The Parliament was limited to a consultative role (reminiscent of its original role as the Assembly), while the Commission's role was limited to the non-executive right of initiative. As Pillars II and III do not produce legally binding acts (i.e. the law of the EU is contained within the 'EC pillar'), the ECJ was left with virtually no role to play under those pillars.

As with the SEA before it, the TEU has been the subject of considerable academic analysis and criticism, not all of it complimentary.

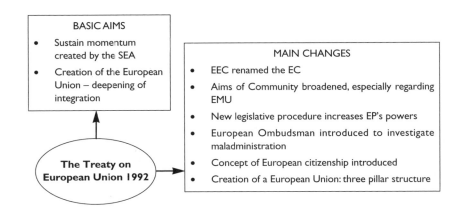

BASIC AIMS
- Sustain momentum created by the SEA
- Creation of the European Union – deepening of integration

The Treaty on European Union 1992

MAIN CHANGES
- EEC renamed the EC
- Aims of Community broadened, especially regarding EMU
- New legislative procedure increases EP's powers
- European Ombudsman introduced to investigate maladministration
- Concept of European citizenship introduced
- Creation of a European Union: three pillar structure

Commentators claim, for example, that the structure of the Union is too complex and fragmented and that the 'opt-outs' available provide for loss of unity (e.g. the UK's reluctance to join the single currency). On the other hand, the Treaty has also been praised for measures such as increasing the role of the Parliament, widening the areas of European competence and increased flexibility.

4. The Treaty of Amsterdam 1997

The Treaty of Amsterdam (ToA), which came into effect in May 1999, has been described as a consolidating Treaty, its main purposes being to improve processes, increase effectiveness and to bring the EU closer to the ordinary person by making it more comprehensible.

Its general provisions, that is, those that affect all three Pillars, include a commitment to greater openness in the decision-making processes of the EU (transparency) and the recognition that the Union is based on respect for fundamental rights, democracy and the rule of law. Indeed, membership of the Union is now contingent upon respect for such principles and the Treaty goes as far as to declare that the Union must respect the human rights protected under the European Convention on Human Rights. Any Member State found to be in 'serious and persistent' breach of such rights may find its own rights, particularly those in regard to voting, suspended.

The ToA transferred a number of areas previously contained in Pillar III to Pillar I. These areas include issues relating to free movement of persons such as visas, asylum and immigration and also customs co-operation. (It is important to note that the United Kingdom and Ireland negotiated an 'opt-out', failing to sign the 1985 Schengen Treaty on the abolition of border checks.) This has resulted in issues relating to the establishment of 'an area of freedom, justice and security' being contained within both Pillars I and III, which has, in turn, led to a blurring of the pillars and also of the role of institutions, particularly the EP and the ECJ.

With regard to Pillar I (the Communities), under the ToA, the EC Treaty was 'tidied up', with all obsolete provisions being removed. This resulted in an almost complete renumbering of the Treaty and students need to ensure that they know whether Treaty Articles referred to in journals and books relate to the old or new system of numbering. (Note that anything published before 1999 is likely to refer to the 'old' numbering of the EC Treaty.)

Specific changes to the EC Treaty included a new non-discrimination provision that provides the EC with the authority to create secondary legislation aimed at combating discrimination based on sex, racial or ethnic origin, religion or belief, disability, age and/or sexual orientation. Member

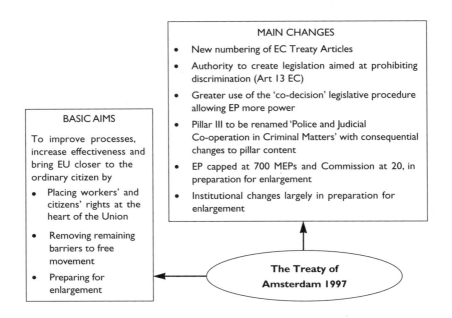

BASIC AIMS

To improve processes, increase effectiveness and bring EU closer to the ordinary citizen by

- Placing workers' and citizens' rights at the heart of the Union

- Removing remaining barriers to free movement

- Preparing for enlargement

MAIN CHANGES

- New numbering of EC Treaty Articles

- Authority to create legislation aimed at prohibiting discrimination (Art 13 EC)

- Greater use of the 'co-decision' legislative procedure allowing EP more power

- Pillar III to be renamed 'Police and Judicial Co-operation in Criminal Matters' with consequential changes to pillar content

- EP capped at 700 MEPs and Commission at 20, in preparation for enlargement

- Institutional changes largely in preparation for enlargement

The Treaty of Amsterdam 1997

States were also encouraged to work together to combat unemployment, while issues such as public health and consumer protection were amended.

With regard to the institutions, the EP was allowed yet further involvement in the legislative process as the use of the co-decision procedure, included by virtue of the TEU, was expanded and simplified.

In an attempt to stem some of the criticisms levied at the original Pillars II and III, a number of changes were made to their structure. These largely related to procedures, financing, institutional involvement and international identity, together with a revision of the defence provisions. With regard to Pillar III, a substantial part of the subject matter of the Pillar was incorporated into Pillar I, where it was included in the EC Treaty. Pillar III was also renamed Police and Judicial Co-operation in Criminal Matters with areas targeted for 'common action' including terrorism, drugs and arms trafficking, trafficking in persons, offences against children, corruption, fraud and the prevention and combating of racism and xenophobia.

5. The Treaty of Nice 2000

The Treaty of Nice (ToN), which came into effect in February 2003, was created with the aim of facilitating, largely through institutional reform, the enlargement of the EU.

The changes introduced by Nice have been described as 'modest' and even 'disappointing' and it has been argued that important issues such as the future of the Common Agricultural Policy and how power should, in future, be divided by the Member States and Community were largely ignored, with other significant decisions, such as the status of the Charter on Fundamental Rights (see Chapter 4), being put off until the Intergovernmental Conference (IGC) of 2004.

The key points agreed at Nice can, however, be summarised as follows:

The decision-making process. This is an extension of qualified majority voting within the Council and a consequent decline in the requirement of unanimity. In addition, the procedure was changed, in that any decision now needs to receive a specified number of votes (the 'threshold') *together with* the approval of a majority of Member States. Member States may also request verification that an agreement represents at least 62 per cent of the total population of the EU. There was also a re-weighting of the votes in favour of the larger EU countries and the use of the co-decision procedure was increased, allowing the EP additional legislative authority.

The legal system. In order to limit delays in obtaining judgements of the ECJ, changes relating to the composition of 'chambers' were initiated, together with a redistribution of responsibilities between the Courts, allowing the CFI to provide preliminary rulings (discussed in Chapter 6) on specific matters.

Other institutional changes. The Commission was allowed to increase in size to a maximum of 27 commissioners, with larger States losing their

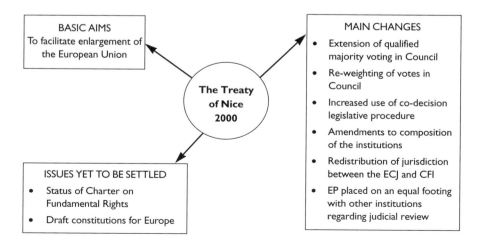

second commissioner. The nomination of Commission President, who now enjoys increased powers, lies in the hands of the Council, with the need for approval from the EP. The EP increased in size to a maximum of 732 MEPs and was also placed on an equal footing with the Council and Commission with regard to the instigation of proceedings under Art 230 EC (also discussed further in Chapter 6). Finally, the size of CoA was also increased to one representative from each Member State, with the Economic and Social Committee and the Committee of Regions increasing in size to a maximum of 350 members apiece.

6. Enlargement of the EEC/EC/EU

i. *Britain's membership of the Communities*

By the early 1960s, the Member States of the Communities were beginning to enjoy the benefits of membership. A number of non-member European States, in particular the United Kingdom, were becoming aware of the apparent benefits of membership and, in 1961, Britain made its first application to join. General De Gaulle, the then President of France, made no secret of his hostility towards British membership, feeling instead that the United Kingdom should continue its association with the Commonwealth and the United States. Britain's application was consequently rejected.

A second UK bid to join in 1967 also failed and it was not until January 1973, following De Gaulle's resignation, that the United Kingdom (together with Ireland and Denmark) was finally admitted.

7. Further broadening of membership of the EC/EU

In 1981, Greece joined the Communities, with Portugal and Spain raising the number of Member States to 12 by 1986. Austria, Sweden and Finland joined in January 1995, bringing the total to 15 Member States.

In May 2004, a further 10 States joined the Union, namely the former eastern bloc countries of Estonia, the Czech Republic, Latvia, Lithuania, Hungary, Poland, Slovenia and Slovakia, together with Cyprus and Malta.

Gunter Verheugen, the Commissioner for Enlargement concluded that the latest enlargement of the EU 'is a further step towards the fulfilment of a ideal that will bring peace, stability and democracy to the whole area ranging from the Baltic Sea to the Black Sea', which demonstrates that the original goals for Europe are as relevant today as they were over half a century ago.

8. Plans for further enlargement

Bulgaria and Romania are set to join in 2007, while uncertainty remains over the inclusion of Turkey, a further applicant, as it has not yet been judged as meeting the criteria for membership. (Article 49 TEU sets out both the criteria and process for membership and is consequently essential reading.)

9. A constitution for Europe?

Debate on creating a constitution for Europe is not a new issue and the prospect has been considered at various times since the mid-1970s, with the most recent discussions culminating in the Heads of State or Government of the Member States agreeing the text of a 'Treaty establishing a Constitution for Europe' in 2004.

In 2001, the Heads of State met at Laeken, Belgium for an IGC. *(Remember to look up any unfamiliar abbreviations or terms in the list of abbreviations/glossary at the beginning of this book!)* In what has become known as the Laeken Declaration, the challenges facing the EU were set out. It was recognised, in particular, that the institutions needed to bring themselves closer to the peoples of Europe by increasing democracy, transparency and efficiency, while the EU's role on the global stage was also in need of clarification.

The European Council, through the Laeken Declaration, set up a 'European Convention' to consider these challenges, including the status of the EU's Charter of Fundamental Rights, and also to draft a Constitution for Europe. The Convention was a move away from the norm – that is, discussion behind closed doors – to a far more public debate. Composed of 105 members representing the governments of the Member and candidate States, national parliaments and the European Parliament and Commission, the proceedings were overseen by observers representing the Committee of Regions (CoR), the Economic and Social Committee (ECOSOC) and the European Ombudsman. Debates were also open to the public, as were all official documents. In addition, the Convention set up numerous working groups and consulted with interested parties such as trade unions, employers' organisations and academics.

In 2003, after 16 months of intensive work, the European Convention produced a draft treaty establishing a *Constitution for Europe* (The Constitutional Treaty or CT). This draft treaty was submitted to an IGC and, in October 2004, was *unanimously agreed* and signed by the Heads of State or Government of all 25 Member States and the 3 candidate countries.

However, before the Treaty establishing a Constitution for Europe can enter into force, it has to be *ratified by all Member States*. The ratification process must be conducted in accordance with the constitutional procedures of each Member State. During 2005 the peoples of France and the Netherlands rejected the text of the Constitution. In the light of this, the European Council has provided that while the ratification process has not been abandoned, the timetable for the introduction of the CT – which was to take place in November 2006 – has had to be 'adjusted'.

While commentators have seriously questioned whether the Constitutional Treaty will now take effect at all, at least in its present form, the mood of the leaders of the Member States appears to have been summed up by a German spokesperson, who provided that *'the no vote leaves the European Union without the political and legal structures needed for an union of 25 members'* and further questions are likely to be asked on the direction that the European project is now likely to take.

In view of the uncertain position of the CT and future changes to the EU, do ensure that you keep up to date with developments by regularly visiting the Europa website, reading a 'good' newspaper and by researching appropriate legal journals for discussion on the way forward.

i. Contents of the CT

While it may appear to be rather a waste of time considering the contents of a document which is now unlikely to come into effect, at least in its present form, the CT can give us important clues as to possible ways forward for the EU. For this reason, a brief overview of the CT has been provided.

THE CONSTITUTIONAL TREATY

The CT was divided into four main parts. Following a Preamble, which recalls the history and heritage of Europe, Part I set out the principles, objectives and institutional provisions of the 'new' EU. Part II comprised the European Charter of Fundamental Rights, while

Part III set out the provisions governing the policies and functioning, both internal and external, of the Union. Finally, Part IV dealt with issues such as the entry into force of the new Treaty, procedures for its revision and also for the repeal of the earlier Treaties.

The Europa website lists the main innovations contained in the CT as follows:

The founding principles of the Union

- The values and objectives of the Union are enshrined, as are the rights of European citizens, thanks to the incorporation into the Constitution of the European Charter of Fundamental Rights.

- The Union is accorded a single legal personality (merger of the EC with the EU).

- The competences (exclusive, shared and supporting) and their distribution between the Member States and the Union are defined clearly and permanently.

- For the first time, with the introduction of a voluntary withdrawal clause, Member States may withdraw from the Union.

- The instruments of action available to the Union are simplified, reducing their number from 15 to 6, as is the terminology, with the introduction of European laws and European framework laws.

- For the first time, the democratic underpinnings of the Union, including participatory democracy, are defined, and a genuine right of popular legislative initiative is introduced.

The institutions

- The seats in the EP are distributed on a degressively proportional basis.

- The European Council, which will be chaired by a President elected for two and a half years, is formally institutionalised, and the rotating Presidency of the European Council is discarded.

- The size of the Commission will be reduced from 2014, to make the number of Commissioners equal to two-thirds of the number of Member States.

- The President of the Commission is to be elected by the EP based on a proposal from the European Council.

- A Minister for Foreign Affairs is to be appointed, taking over the tasks of the External Relations Commissioner and the High Representative for the Common Foreign and Security Policy attached to the Council.

Decision making

- A new qualified majority system is established under which 55 per cent of the Member States representing 65 per cent of the population will constitute a qualified majority.
- Qualified majority voting in the Council of Ministers is being extended to cover around 20 existing and 20 new legal bases.
- The joint adoption of European laws and framework laws by the EP and the Council is to become the norm (ordinary legislative procedure).
- Several bridging clauses are created for facilitating subsequent extensions of qualified majority voting and switchover to the ordinary legislative procedure.

Union policies

- Economic co-ordination between the countries that have adopted the euro is to be improved, and the informal role of the Euro Group is to be recognised.
- The pillar structure is abolished. The second (common foreign and security policy) and third (justice and home affairs) pillars, which were hitherto subject to the intergovernmental method, are brought within the Community framework.
- The common foreign and security policy is strengthened with the creation of a European Minister for Foreign Affairs and the progressive definition of a common defence policy through, for example, the creation of a European Defence Agency and the authorisation of enhanced co-operation in this field.
- A genuine area of freedom, security and justice is to be created through the planned implementation of common policies on asylum, immigration and external border control, in the field of judicial and police co-operation and through the development of Europol and Eurojust actions and the creation of a European Public Prosecutor's Office.

III. THE EU TODAY

It should be evident by this stage that the EU is a complex structure. The Member States, while subscribing to the idea of an integrated Europe, do not always agree on the extent of such integration or on the means by which it should be achieved, and the issue of subsidiarity – or how competences are divided between the Member States and the EU Institutions – continues to be a major issue. The original European Community, the ECSC, created in 1952, was designed as a first step in achieving lasting peace and increasing prosperity in a continent scarred by war. These aims have, by and large, been achieved: half a century of peace together with the status of being one of the three most prosperous areas of the world are surely achievements to be proud of. However, the aims and objectives of the Union are constantly developing in response to both internal and external stimuli and the integration of Europe is far from complete.

The recent enlargement of the Union has itself presented significant challenges. The ambitious target of introducing a single currency throughout the Union, for example, continues to remain at the top of any European agenda. In addition, a further broadening of the Union to include yet more new states, namely Bulgaria and Rumania in 2007, together with a deepening of European integration to include both wider political and social issues presents yet further challenges, as does the issue of democratic legitimacy in Europe. The protection of Fundamental Rights (discussed briefly in Chapter 4) and the appropriate status of EU Charter of Fundamental Rights (not to be confused with the European Convention for the Protection of Human Rights and Fundamental Freedoms (ECHR)) is a further dilemma yet to be solved.

Add to this the Union's attempts at establishing a global identity and your head is likely to be left reeling with the enormity of the tasks which lie ahead for Europe!

Important dates and events in the creation of a EU:

Apr 1951   Six European States sign the Treaty of Paris establishing the ECSC

Mar 1957   The six sign the Treaties of Rome establishing Euratom and the EEC

Jan 1958   Treaties of Rome come into force

Apr 1965	Merger Treaty is signed providing all three Communities with the same institutional structure
Jul 1967	Merger Treaty enters into force
Apr 1970	First Budgetary Treaty signed, making major changes to the funding of the Communities
Jan 1973	Denmark, Ireland and the United Kingdom join the Community
Dec 1974	Agreement on direct elections to the EP – a major step in ensuring a democratic Europe
Jul 1975	Second Budgetary Treaty signed
Jul 1978	European Council agrees on closer monetary co-operation
Jun 1979	First direct elections to the EP
Jan 1981	Greece joins the Community
Jan 1986	Spain and Portugal join the Community
Feb 1986	SEA signed with the aim of speeding up European integration
Jul 1987	SEA enters into force
Feb 1992	TEU signed in Maastricht – creates a European Union
Nov 1993	TEU enters into force
Jan 1995	Austria, Finland and Sweden join the Union
Oct 1997	ToA signed – consolidating Treaty aimed at enlargement and bringing EU closer to its citizens
May 1999	ToA enters into force
Dec 2000	ToN signed
Feb 2003	ToN enters into force
May 2004	Estonia, the Czech Republic, Latvia, Lithuania, Hungary, Poland, Slovenia, Slovakia, Cyprus and Malta join the EU
June 2004	25 Member States unanimously adopt the Treaty establishing a Constitution for Europe
June 2004	France and Holland reject the text of the Constitutional Treaty

3 Who Runs Europe?

I. POWER SHARING

Since the first European Community (the ECSC) was created, the Member States have delegated powers to a number of supranational institutions who 'run' the Communities on their behalf. Together, these institutions fulfil the functions of government of the Community, taking decisions, creating laws and spending money on a joint (Community), rather than individual (State) basis, but only in areas in which they have been provided with the authority to do so. The Member States still retain the power to create and amend the constitutional rules of the EU, as has been done through a variety of Treaties, such as the TEU, the ToA and the ToN, and they continue to be solely responsible in areas that lie outside the competence of the EC.

Over the past 50 years, numerous theories of integration have been put forward in an attempt to explain how power is, or should be, shared between the Member States and the institutions. Federalism has proved a tremendous influence on the governance of the EC. Although there is no precise agreed definition of federalism, and a cursory examination of various federal systems throughout the world reveals that there are many different models, it basically means that there is a dispersal of power between different levels of government.

Federalist ideas are evident throughout the Treaties, with great emphasis being placed on the EC institutions which enjoy a large degree of autonomy in specific fields. A federalist principle that has proved important to the EC is that of subsidiarity. The principle, which was given formal recognition by the TEU, can now be found in Art 5 EC. It provides that decisions relating to areas where the Community and the Member States have joint competence to act should be taken at the most appropriate level, as close to the citizen as possible, providing there is no loss of effectiveness. This demonstrates that power is intended to be shared between the supranational institutions, national (Member State) and sub-national (regional) levels.The idea of a federal Europe has, however, not proved popular with all Member States, the United Kingdom included, due to the necessity of surrendering sovereignty, albeit in limited fields.

An alternative theory of integration is that of intergovernmentalism (see Glossary). Intergovernmentalism has been criticised due to its tendency to promote the interests of individual States, rather than Europe as a whole, and also due to the difficulties often encountered in reaching agreement between the Member States. The EU can be seen as embracing both theories of integration. While Pillar I (EC) relies largely on its supranational institutions to take decisions that bind the Member States, decisions relating to Pillars II and III are made by the Member States acting together on an intergovernmental basis, with limited involvement from the institutions other than the Council.

II. THE INSTITUTIONAL STRUCTURE

1. The institutions and other Community bodies

Article 7 EC provides that the tasks entrusted to the Community shall be carried out by five institutions, namely the EP, the Council, the Commission, the ECJ and the CoA. The Treaties have also provided for the establishment of several additional bodies such as the European Council, the ECOSOC and the CoR. As the Communities have grown and developed into the EU, so, too, have the institutions grown and developed. In order to ensure that no one body becomes too powerful, thereby disturbing the delicate balance that exists between the various interests within the Union, a number of checks and balances are inbuilt into the EU's system of governance.

In order to understand the workings of the institutions, each will be considered separately in terms of the role that it plays and also with regard to its relationship with the other institutions.

2. The functions of government

It is worth taking a moment to remind ourselves of the traditional division of government functions, that is, legislative, executive and judicial. In the United Kingdom, an attempt is made at keeping each area separate, in order to check the potential for arbitrary government. No such division is attempted in Europe and the roles of government are shared, rather than divided, amongst the Institutions. It is not possible, therefore, to declare any single institution as, for example, the legislator of the EU.

3. The European Parliament (Arts 189–201 EC)

i. Composition and functions of the Parliament

The EP (or Assembly, as it was officially known prior to the SEA) was created under the ECSC Treaty in 1952. It consisted of 78 members who were delegates of their own national parliaments, representing political rather than national affiliations. While the role of a parliament traditionally involves a substantial legislative function, the EP was initially limited to an advisory role, providing little more than a forum for debate.

The EP is composed of a maximum of 732 members (known as MEPs) who, since 1979, have been directly elected via democratic elections held every five years in each Member State. It is the largest multinational parliament in the world, presently representing the interests of approximately 500 million EU citizens. It sits in Strasbourg for monthly plenary sessions and holds committee meetings and additional sessions in Brussels, while its General Secretariat is based in Luxembourg. All of the EU's major political parties are represented and MEPs are grouped together according to their political affiliations, rather than by nationality.

The work of the EP, much of it done through committees, can be divided into three main areas:

- legislative
- budgetary
- supervisory.

Each of these powers will be considered in turn.

The legislative role of the EP

The legislative processes of the EC are complicated and normally involve the participation of three of the EC's institutions: the Commission, whose role is largely to propose and draft legislation; the Council, which must normally provide their assent before legislation can take effect; and the Parliament, whose role varies depending on the subject matter of the proposed legislation. It is important to understand that not only are there different forms of EC legislation (most importantly, regulations, directives and decisions), but also that there are a number of different processes by which legislation may be enacted. The main legislative procedures are as follows.

Consultation – As already touched upon, the Parliament was originally provided with a purely consultative role with regard to the creation of EC legislation. In order to distinguish this process from other legislative procedures, it has become known as the 'consultation procedure'. This procedure requires that, before legislation may be adopted, the EP must be consulted. While neither the Council nor the Commission is required to act on any opinions or proposals for change put forward by the EP, failure to consult can lead to legislation being declared void by the ECJ (Case 138/79, *Roquette Frères v Council*). The procedure is now rarely used, having been superseded by new procedures that have strengthened Parliament's legislative powers.

Co-operation – Consideration of the ECSC Treaty demonstrates that, from the outset, it had been intended that the EP should eventually become elected by universal suffrage. It was not until 1974, however, in a meeting of the European Council, that it was decided that such elections should take place as 'soon as possible'. As a corollary to this, it was added that the powers of the Parliament should also be extended, particularly with regard to the Community's legislative processes. Direct elections have, without a doubt, given the EP greater legitimacy and authority and, as a result of calls for increased powers for the EP, the SEA introduced a new procedure to be known as 'co-operation'. This is seen as being a first step in the extension of the powers of the democratically elected Parliament. Under this rather complicated procedure, the EP may reject draft legislation, which the Council may only subsequently adopt by unanimity, rather than the more usual QMV.

While still not placing the EP on an equal footing with the Council in the legislative process, the procedure increased Parliament's influence, resulting in both the Council and the Commission becoming more inclined to take into consideration the EP's points of view. It should be remembered, however, that following the SEA, the consultation procedure was still very much the norm and that the new co-operation procedure was limited in its application to relatively few areas.

Assent – In addition, the SEA also introduced a procedure known as the 'assent procedure', giving the EP the right of veto with regard to decisions of a non-routine legislative nature. This has been used in areas such as the accession of new Member States and agreements with non-Member States, where the EP must provide its agreement before the Council can adopt a draft proposal from the Commission. The TEU has since made some changes to this procedure and also extended it to all international agreements.

Co-decision – The TEU further increased the EP's legislative powers by introducing a procedure known as 'co-decision'. The main difference between the co-decision and co-operation procedures is that the former allows the EP to veto, by absolute majority, a proposed legislative measure. The importance of the procedure from the Parliament's point of view is that it allows the EP to prevent the Council from passing legislation without its agreement. It is important, however, to note that the use of the co-decision was again limited, the co-operation procedure becoming the norm under the TEU. The ToA and ToN have since extended the use of co-decision, which has had the effect of increasing the influence of the EP in the Community's legislative process.

The Parliament's budgetary role

Initially, the EP had, in line with its legislative powers, a purely consultative role in relation to the Community's budget. In 1970, major changes were made with regard to the funding of the Communities and this coincided with the first major extension of the EP's powers via the 1970 and 1975 Budgetary Treaties.

Four institutions have a part to play in the Community's budgetary process. The Commission is responsible for drawing up a draft budget, which the Council and Parliament adopt, while the CoA provides an annual audit. A draft budget will contain details of proposed compulsory and non-compulsory expenditure and also an estimate of revenue. The Parliament has the power to amend the sections of the budget relating to non-compulsory expenditure, but may only suggest amendments with regard to compulsory expenditure, as the Council has the final say in this area. Parliament does, however, have the power to reject a draft budget in its entirety and has done so on a number of occasions. When this happens, the Community must proceed on the basis of the previous year's budget until agreement can be reached.

The EP's budgetary role can therefore be described as substantial, but should not be overestimated as, first, the largest share of the budget is compulsory and therefore largely controlled by the Council and, second, the EP has no control over revenue raising.

The Parliament's supervisory role

As there is no separation of the powers of government within the EC, the EC Treaty provides for a number of 'checks and balances' to ensure that no one institution can become too powerful. As part of this system of checks and balances, the institutions all play a part in supervising each other.

The Parliament and the Commission – One of the more important supervisory powers held by the EP is that which it has over the Commission. Under the ECSC Treaty, the Parliament (then the Assembly) was entitled to debate the annual report produced by the Commission (then the High Authority). Provided a two-thirds majority could be achieved, the EP could pass a motion of censure, requiring the Commission to resign en bloc. This power is still enjoyed by the Parliament but, to date, has never been used, probably because it has been seen as far too severe a sanction to impose and, also, in most circumstances, the EP and the Commission consider themselves allies rather than adversaries. Also, until amendments were introduced by the TEU, the EP was unable to exert control over the appointment of new Commissioners and it would therefore have been rather pointless to sack the Commission when it had no control over who was to replace the outgoing Commissioners.

The Parliament and the Council – The ECSC Treaty also provided that the EP may request that the Commission reply to oral or written questions put by it. In 1973, the Parliament made time in its schedule for a regular 'question time' with regard to both the Commission and the Council. While this power may be effective as a means of exposing wrongdoing, the Council, unlike the Commission, cannot be forced to reply to the Parliament's questioning and neither is there any sanction available against it.

The Parliamentary Ombudsman and maladministration – The EP may set up committees of inquiry to investigate allegations of maladministration. The TEU also provided that the EP may appoint an Ombudsman to receive complaints regarding possible maladministration against any EU body, received either directly from citizens or via an MEP. In addition, the Ombudsman may initiate inquiries on his own initiative. At the conclusion of an investigation, the Ombudsman is required to report to the EP, which has no powers to correct the situation, but the process allows such maladministration to be brought to the attention of the media.

The Parliament and judicial review – The EP may exert supervisory powers over the law-making powers of the other institutions by instituting a legal challenge before the ECJ. This procedure, known as 'judicial review' (Art 230 EC, discussed in Chapter 6), provides that the Parliament may challenge legally effective Acts (largely secondary legislation) produced by the other institutions. It may similarly, under Art 232 EC, challenge the other institutions should they fail to act when bound to do so by

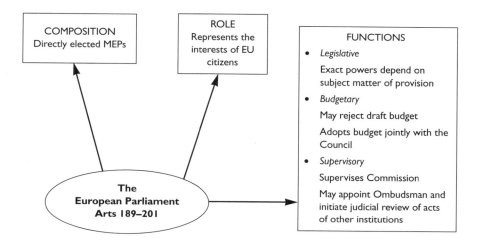

Community rules. It was originally thought that the Parliament lacked locus standi to make a challenge (as can be evidenced by Case 302/87, *European Parliament v Council*, the *Comitology* case), however, in the later *Chernobyl* case (Case C-70/88, *European Parliament v Council*), the ECJ declared that the Parliament might bring such an action in circumstances where it was acting to protect its 'prerogatives'. The EC Treaty was later amended by the SEA, which formally acknowledged this right. The ToN has since increased the EP's role, which is now comparable to that of the Commission and the Council.

Conclusions – It can be concluded that the powers of the Parliament, although initially weak, have substantially increased over time, largely as a result of its being directly and democratically elected. It can be argued that this is only right and proper, as it is the EP which enjoys the mandate of the peoples of Europe and to continue to deny the Parliament a proper voice in Europe would have been to ignore the concept of democracy.

4. The Council of the European Union (Arts 202–10 EC)

i. The composition of the Council

The Council of Ministers or, as it has been formally known since the TEU, the Council of the European Union, is comprised of one representative from each Member State, authorised to bind the government of that State. The composition of the Council at any one time will depend on the subject matter under discussion: for example, if the Council is discussing matters relating to agriculture, each Member State's agriculture minister will be present. Similarly, if transport matters are under discussion, transport ministers will attend.

The Council is led by a president, with the presidency rotating between the Member States on a six-monthly basis. It is the Member State holding the presidency that decides what will be discussed and when.

ii. The Committee of Permanent Representatives (COREPER)

The Council ministers are supported by permanent representatives of the Member States (known collectively as the Committee of Permanent Representatives (COREPER)). COREPER consists of senior diplomats and it is instructive to note that it has been suggested that 90 per cent of all EU decisions are actually taken by COREPER before they even reach ministerial level!

In addition to COREPER, the Council also has a General Secretariat providing administrative support.

iii. The role of the Council

The Council represents national interests and, as a body, has characteristics of both a supranational and intergovernmental organisation. The ministers who form the Council are responsible to their national parliaments, yet they form part of the institutional body that makes decisions on behalf of Europe. The EC Treaty provides that the function of the Council is to 'ensure that the objectives set out in the Treaty are attained'.

iv. The Council's legislative role

Originally, the Council was considered to be the principal legislator for the Community. Since developments wrought by the amending Treaties, the Council now shares its legislative role, although not equally, with the European Parliament, with whom it also shares budgetary powers.

The Council's legislative powers can be summarised thus:

- the right to approve draft legislation placed before it by the Commission after the proper involvement of the EP;

- the right (under Art 208 EC) to request that the Commission undertakes various studies and, as a result, submits proposals;

- the right to delegate legislative power to the Commission in areas where specific or detailed rules are required.

v. Reaching agreement in the Council

In addition to its legislative powers, the Council sets political objectives, co-ordinates national policies and provides a forum where differences between Member States may be resolved. When the Council is required to reach a decision – whether it relates to legislation or another matter – it does so by taking a vote. There are three systems of voting that may be used: simple majority, qualified majority or unanimity. Reaching a decision by simple majority simply requires that the majority of Council ministers

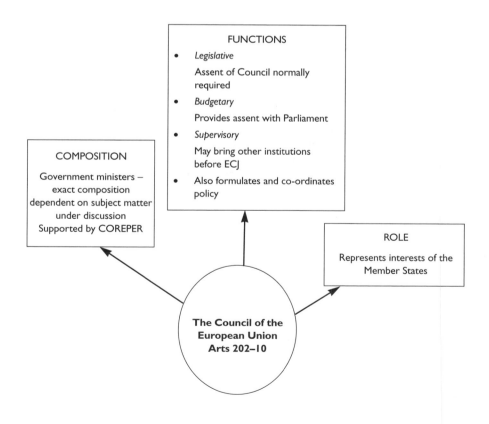

support a proposal. This requires Member States to surrender a high degree of sovereignty and is consequently rarely used.

Initially, the favoured method of voting was unanimity, effectively allowing each Member State the power of veto. While this method is still used in restricted areas, QMV has become the norm. Under this method, each Member State's vote is 'weighted' to reflect the size of its population (Art 205 EC). Changes wrought under the ToN also require that, the decision receives at least a specified number of votes (known as the 'threshold') and is approved by the majority of Member States. In addition, any member of the Council may request verification that the qualified majority represents at least 62 per cent of the total population of the EU. This method of reaching decisions means that a Member State may find itself bound by a decision which it does not approve of.

vi. The Luxembourg Accords

When, in 1966, the Council moved towards the regular use of QMV, France refused to attend Council meetings (known as the 'empty chair' policy), objecting to the resulting loss of sovereignty. This protest resulted in what has become known as the Luxembourg Compromise (or Accords), when it was agreed that, should a decision be required on an issue relating to 'very important interests' of a Member State, that State would be treated as having a right of veto. This had the effect of increasing the power of the Council, which represents Member State interests, and decreasing the influence of the Commission, which represents the interests of the Community as a whole. The effect of this 'veto' should not be overemphasised, however, as, before it may be evoked, a Member State must successfully demonstrate that the issue in question relates to sufficiently important interests and it is seen very much as a measure of last resort.

vii. Supervisory role

In addition, the Council, in the same manner as the EP and the Commission, exerts supervisory powers over the other institutions by virtue of the judicial review procedures contained in the EC Treaty (discussed in Chapter 6).

5. The European Council

Take care not to confuse the European Council with either the Council of Ministers (or as it is now known, the Council of the European Union) or the Council of Europe (which exists totally outside both the EC and the EU).

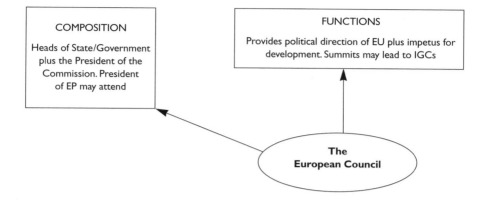

The European Council is composed of the Heads of Government or State of the Member States, together with the Commission President. Regular meetings (known as summits) have been taking place between such Heads since the 1960s, but the decision to formalise such meetings was not taken until much later. While Member States' interests were already represented in the Council of Ministers, it was decided that strategy for the development of the Community should be concluded at the highest possible political level. In addition, it was seen as an appropriate forum for settling disagreements of fundamental importance between Member States.

Despite its rather uncertain institutional status, the European Council has become increasingly important, providing political direction and the impetus for development within Europe. Major changes to the Treaties are, for example, preceded by summit meetings which, in turn, will lead on to an IGC from which amendments to primary legislation will emerge.

It was agreement at European Council level that led to the introduction of direct elections for the EP and also to the creation of a European unit of currency, while the impetus for the EU (as opposed to the EC) was a result of an ad hoc committee set up by the European Council (the Dooge Committee). Other topics regularly debated by the European Council include the state of the European economy and external relations.

The European Council can be seen as an example of the way in which the Community has evolved. While its beginnings can be traced back to a series of ad hoc meetings, it is now recognised and valued as a vitally important decision-making body.

6. The European Commission (Arts 211–19 EC)

The Commission's position within the institutional balance of the Community has varied considerably during its lifetime, fluctuating between being heralded as the embryonic European government and the Community's civil service. The Commission's position within the institutional balance has undoubtedly suffered as a result of the increased power enjoyed by the EP, and the 'Brussels bureaucrats' are seen to be held in low esteem by the general public – at least if the UK's popular press are to be believed. Publicity surrounding the Commission's en bloc resignation in 1999 as a result of allegations of malpractice did little to improve its reputation, despite its commitment to 'transparency' in the exercise of its functions. On the whole, however, the Commission can be seen as a success, as the progress made with regards to European integration could not have been achieved without the institution's input as motivator, monitor and negotiator.

i. The composition of the Commission

The Commission is comprised of up to 27 Commissioners, one from each Member State. Commissioners, who must be EC citizens, are nominated by the governments of the Member States, subject to the approval of the EP. The EC Treaty requires that each Commissioner be independent and Commissioners are required to swear an oath promising not to take instruction from any government or other body and to act only in the interests of the Community. While a Commissioner who fails to fulfil the conditions of his appointment may be dismissed by the ECJ, the EP may also dismiss the Commission en bloc. (It is relevant to note that the involvement of the EP in the appointment of the Commission is considered to be a positive step, thereby increasing its democratic legitimacy.)

The Council of the European Union appoints a President from amongst the Commissioners, after first consulting the EP. This is a particularly influential post, as the President will not only chair Commission meetings and attend the meetings of the European Council, but will also represent Europe at international summits. The Commission is divided into directorates-general (DGs), each headed by a director-general who in turn reports to a Commissioner with overall responsibility for the work of that DG. The DGs are divided by subject matter, for example, industry or matters relating to education, training and youth. Each Commissioner is supported by a cabinet and the Commission has a total staff of approximately 18,000.

ii. The role of the Commission

While the EP represents the interests of the citizens of Europe and the Council represents the interests of the Member States, the Commission represents the interests of the Community as a whole. Article 211 EC provides that the Commission must 'ensure the proper functioning and development of the common market' and this has resulted in the Commission becoming known as the 'Guardian of the Treaties'.

The Commission is a multi-purpose organisation and its functions include the legislative, administrative, executive and quasi-judicial functions as outlined below.

The Commission's legislative role

The Commission plays a central role in the Community's legislative process, its most important function being that of initiator of draft legislation. As has already been discussed above in relation to the EP, the Commission will produce draft legislation which it then sends to the Council and the EP for their consideration and/or approval. The Commission further participates in the legislative process by amending legislative proposals in circumstances where either the Council or Parliament or both have failed to provide the necessary agreement, often reacting to amendments suggested by those institutions.

Many of the Commission's proposals for legislation are a direct result of Council requests that various studies be undertaken (under Art 208 EC) and, since amendments introduced by the TEU, the EP may also request that the Commission submits legislative proposals on appropriate matters (Art 192 EC). The Commission publishes an annual programme outlining its legislative plans and listing legislative priorities for that year, thereby playing a part in planning the strategy for the Community as a whole. In addition, the Commission has been dubbed the 'motor for integration' of the Community, due to its involvement in the development of policy. This can be evidenced by the Commission's White Paper entitled Completion of the Internal Market (COM (85) 310), which was significant in the shaping of the SEA.

The Commission also has the power, in very limited circumstances, to act alone in the making of EC legislation. (This can be evidenced by reference to Art 86(3) EC.) In addition, the Council may delegate legislative powers to the Commission, once again in limited circumstances.

The Commission's administrative and executive roles

Legislation, once enacted, must be implemented and policy, once made, must be put into effect. The Commission's role is generally not one of direct action, as both policy and legislation are largely put into effect at national level, but to maintain a supervisory position, ensuring that the appropriate Member States' agencies comply.

The Commission manages the EU's annual budget, including a number of funds such as the European Social Fund and, importantly, the European Agricultural and Guarantee Fund which takes up approximately 50 per cent of the Community's annual budget.

The Commission also has a central role with regard to the Community's external relations. The EU's effectiveness on a global level is enhanced by the Commission's role as negotiator of trade and co-operation agreements with countries or groups of countries outside the Community. The Commission, for example, represents the EU at the United Nations and its specialised agencies, such as the World Trade Organisation (see Art 302 EC).

The Commission's supervisory and quasi-judicial functions

The Commission has two separate judicial (or quasi-judicial) functions. First, Art 226 EC provides the Commission with the power to investigate,

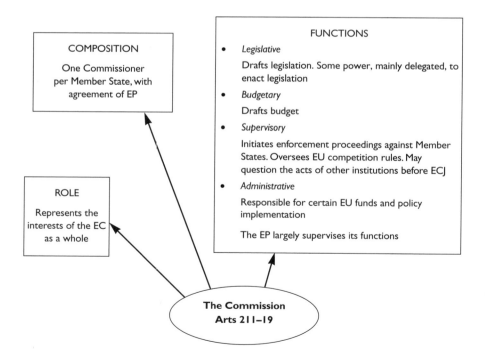

COMPOSITION

One Commissioner
per Member State, with
agreement of EP

ROLE

Represents the
interests of the EC
as a whole

FUNCTIONS

- *Legislative*

  Drafts legislation. Some power, mainly delegated, to enact legislation

- *Budgetary*

  Drafts budget

- *Supervisory*

  Initiates enforcement proceedings against Member States. Oversees EU competition rules. May question the acts of other institutions before ECJ

- *Administrative*

  Responsible for certain EU funds and policy implementation

  The EP largely supervises its functions

The Commission
Arts 211–19

and bring before the ECJ, any Member State that it considers to be in breach of Community obligations. The Commission attempts to remedy any breach as informally as possible, through consultation and negotiation with the errant Member State, and an action before the ECJ is seen very much as a last resort. (This action is discussed in further detail in Chapter 6.)

Second, the Commission plays an important role in ensuring that Community rules relating to competition are followed. For example, any undertaking (the favoured EC term for a firm or individual capable of economic activity) that attempts to distort trade within the Community may find itself in breach of Community law (notably Arts 81 and 82 EC). Under Regulation 17 (1956–62 OJ Spec Ed 87), the Commission was provided with the power to investigate possible breaches, provide formal decisions as to whether there has been an infringement and impose fines against any wrongdoers. While the investigative and forensic powers of the Commission may be subject to judicial review, these functions provide the Commission with significant influence in relation to the development of EC policy.

In addition, the Commission, in the same manner as the EP and Council of the European Union, exerts supervisory powers over the other institutions by virtue of the judicial review procedures contained within the Treaty (discussed in Chapter 6).

Conclusions

It can be concluded that the Commission's functions elevate it far above that of a 'civil service' for the Community. It can be described as a *sui generis*, multi-functional organisation with not inconsiderable influence over not only the day to day running of the Community, but also its development and direction. This said, its powers are not boundless and many are held under the discretion of the Council and the supervision of the EP.

7. The European Court of Justice (Arts 220–45 EC)

The European Communities are founded on the rule of law, and acceptance by the Member States, institutions and individuals of the binding nature of its 'rules' is fundamental to the EC's existence. The role of the ECJ is to 'ensure that in the interpretation and application' of the Treaty, the law is observed (Art 220 EC). Since November 1989, a CFI has assisted the ECJ in its task. Both the ECJ and the CFI sit in Luxembourg.

i. The composition and structure of the ECJ

The ECJ is made up of a number of personnel including judges and advocates general (AGs). While the judges act as the decision makers of the Court, AGs, who have no equivalent in the UK's legal system, assist the judges by delivering non-binding written opinions, which provide advice to the Court prior to its deliberations.

Judges

The number of judges composing the Court is dependent on the number of Member States: one judge per State, for a term of three years, renewable once. The Treaty requires that judges be 'persons whose independence is beyond doubt' and it is clear that judges must be independent of any government or interest group. As with all fixed-term appointments, it is possible that political pressure could be brought to bear on judges. This is reduced, however, as the Court's deliberations are secret, with a single ruling being delivered by the Court rather than individual judgments.

With regard to the qualifications, the Treaty requires that judges must be individuals who 'possess the qualifications required for appointment to the highest judicial offices in their respective countries or who are jurisconsults of recognised competence'. While the United Kingdom has so far chosen to appoint domestic judges or legal practicioners, the Treaty allows academics to be appointed and a number of other States have done so.

Advocates General

In addition to the judges, the ECJ also has a number of AGs, with the rules of appointment and qualifications being the same as those for judges.

ii. The role of the ECJ

The Treaty provides the Court's jurisdiction. The various actions that can be brought before the Court can be divided into direct actions and preliminary rulings. Direct actions include those brought by the Commission against Member States accused of failing to fulfil their Community obligations and actions brought by the institutions or individuals wishing to challenge the validity of Community legislation (both are discussed in further detail in Chapter 6).

Preliminary rulings, on the other hand, are the result of requests by national courts requiring the ECJ to either interpret EC law or rule on the validity of EC secondary legislation. National courts will make such requests when they have a case before them that revolves on a point of Community law (again, see Chapter 6).

In addition to its specific jurisdiction, the Treaty provides that the Court has the rather general function of ensuring the 'law is observed'.

Judicial activism

It has been argued that the ECJ has used this rather broad remit to expand its role beyond that normally performed by a judicial body. The ECJ has adopted a purposive, teleological or contextual, rather than literal, approach to interpreting EC law. As it explained in Case 283/81, *CILFIT*: 'Every provision of Community law must be placed in its context and interpreted in the light of the provisions of Community law as a whole, regard being given to the objectives thereof.' This has allowed the Court to take a major role in filling gaps left by Community legislation which, in turn, has resulted in its being accused of usurping the role of both the Community legislators and policy makers.

Such activism has been denied by both the Court and its supporters, who argue that the ECJ has gone no further than was necessary to give effect to the Treaty, given its nature, which is intended to be no more than a framework.

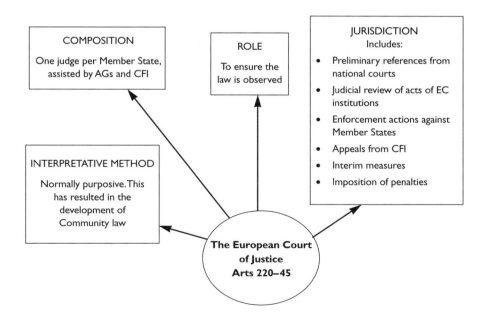

It cannot be denied that the Court has produced some particularly dynamic decisions and one has to look no further than Case 26/62, *Van Gend en Loos*, to see the impact that the Court has had on the development of EC law (see Chapter 5). It has been argued, however, that the ECJ is now playing a far less proactive role, perhaps now content that the Treaty has been sufficiently constitutionalised and the legal order adequately developed.

iii. Procedure before the ECJ

Procedure before the Court can be divided into two stages – oral and written. Unlike the United Kingdom, however, emphasis is placed on written submissions, while the oral stage is limited and short (which is probably advantageous, as the case may be heard in any of the Community's official languages).

The written stage comes first, with relevant documents being communicated to all parties and published in the Official Journal of the European Union. At the end of the written stage, cases may be argued orally in open court and it is following this hearing that the AG will deliver his opinion.

The judges, who may sit in plenary session (all judges) or in chambers, deliberate behind closed doors, delivering their judgement in open court. The judgement, which will be made available in all official languages, will include the reasoning on which it is based. (It is worth noting that the AG's opinion is often very instructive and therefore generally worth reading!)

iv. The Court of First Instance (CFI)

The CFI, which also consists of one judge from each State, was established under the SEA as a means of relieving the excessive workload of the ECJ. The jurisdiction of the Court, which was extended under the ToN, is limited to direct actions and preliminary references on certain specific matters only. Decisions of the CFI may be appealed to the ECJ.

8. The Court of Auditors (Arts 246–48 EC)

The Court was established by the Budgetary Treaty 1975, but it was not until the TEU came into effect that it was afforded the status of Community institution. It is comprised of one member from each Member State. Both the Council and EP are involved in the appointment procedure and auditors must be appropriately qualified and their independence beyond doubt.

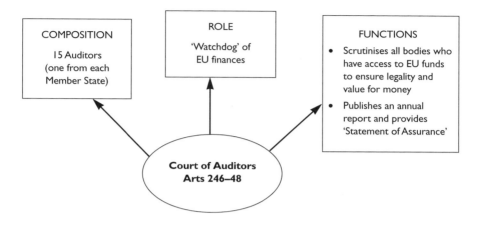

While the CoA has been afforded the title of 'court', its function is not judicial. It is rather the taxpayer's representative, a 'watchdog' over the EU's money and, as the Union's budget has increased, so has the prominence of the Court, although it still remains 'low-key' compared to the other four institutions. Every institution and body that has access to Union funds is subject to the scrutiny of the CoA and the Court provides a check that all legal requirements are observed and also that the Community is receiving value for money.

The CoA publishes an annual report, highlighting any areas where improvements are possible or desirable. The Court also provides the EP and the Council with a Statement of Assurance, which declares that EU money has been spent for the purposes intended.

9. Other Community bodies

The EC Treaty also makes provision for a number of other bodies, the main ones of which will be considered, briefly, in turn.

i. The Economic and Social Committee (ESC)

The ESC is a consultative body which represents a variety of sectional interests. Its membership consists of up to 350 representatives drawn from a broad cross-section of European society, such as workers, employees, farmers, craftsmen, professionals, consumer groups and so on. Meetings are held on a monthly basis.

The EC Treaty requires that draft legislation, in specific policy areas, be referred to the Committee and that the majority of new EC laws of any significance are adopted only following input from the ESC.

ii. The Committee of Regions (CoR)

The CoR was established by the TEU to represent regional and local interests. Like the ESC, it has a membership of up to 350, drawn from around the Member States, and must be consulted by the Council and Commission where the EC Treaty so specifies.

As national barriers break down and borders between the Member States become more open as a consequence of the EC's single market, the creation of a CoR can be seen as a response to people's fears over centralisation. The CoR has direct experience of how EU policies affect the everyday life of citizens and its expertise allows it to bring a powerful influence to bear.

iii. The European System of Central Banks (ESCB) and the European Central Bank (ECB)

The TEU provided a legal basis for Economic and Monetary Union (EMU) and, as part of the third stage of EMU, the ESCB and ECB were created with the primary aim of maintaining price stability (Art 105 EC). The ESCB is composed of the ECB and the national central banks of Member States participating in monetary union. The Treaty provides that 'the ESCB shall support the general economic policies in the Community', providing this does not conflict with the pursuit of price stability.

iv. European Investment Bank (EIB)

The EIB, whose membership comprises the Member States, is the EU's financing institution, providing long-term loans for capital investments which promote the Community's economic development and integration. It supports regional development and its loans are often accompanied by grants from the EU's Structural and Cohesion Funds.

III. ISSUES OF DEMOCRACY AND THE 'INSTITUTIONAL BALANCE'

As can be seen from the above discussions, each of the institutions of the EC represents different interests and has differing functions. It is consequently vital that the powers and influence of each are carefully balanced in order that no one institution – or interest – becomes too powerful.

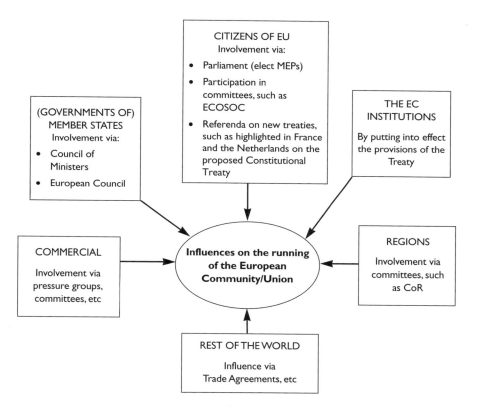

4 Community Law

In order to develop an understanding of European law, its sources need to be examined. Community law can be divided into two categories: primary and secondary. The primary source of EC law is the various Treaties, both those that were enacted in order to create the European Communities and also those that have been enacted in order to amend the original Treaties. (An overview of the main Treaties is provided in Chapter 2.)

Secondary sources include secondary legislation, as enacted by the institutions of the Community, case law, which is derived from the judgments of the ECJ, general principles as 'declared' by the ECJ and international agreements entered into by the Community. Each of these sources will be considered in turn.

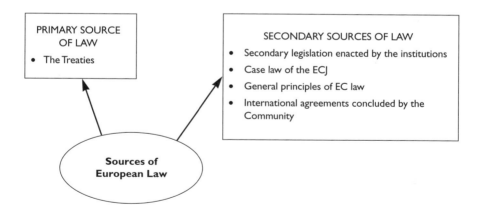

I. PRIMARY SOURCES OF EC LAW

As already touched upon, the principal source of law for the European Communities is the Treaties that created those Communities, namely:

- the Treaty establishing the European Coal and Steel Community 1951 (also known as the Treaty of Paris or the ECSC Treaty);
- the Treaty establishing the European Atomic Energy Community 1957 (the First Treaty of Rome or the Euratom Treaty);
- the Treaty establishing the European Economic Community 1957 (also known as the Treaty of Rome and the EEC Treaty, but now known as the EC Treaty).

The most important Treaty from the point of the European Community is, of course, the last of these. There have also been a number of Treaties enacted which have amended this Treaty and these include the following:

- the Merger Treaty 1965;
- the Budgetary Treaties 1970 and 1975;
- the Single European Act (SEA) 1986;
- the Treaty on European Union (TEU) 1992 (also known as the Maastricht Treaty)*;
- the Treaty of Amsterdam (ToA) 1997;
- the Treaty of Nice (ToN) 2000.

* It should be noted that the TEU could be included in either list as not only did it amend the EC Treaty, but it also created the EU.

The Treaties, along with secondary legislation are divided into 'articles', which are basically the same as 'sections' in UK legislation. They are written thus: Art 249 EC, with last few letters demonstrating which legislative act the article is contained in.

1. Creating primary legislation

The European Council has become pivotal to the initiation of any new treaty. The process generally involves the Council concluding, at a summit meeting, that an IGC is needed in order to discuss any reforms or amendments that may prove necessary. For amendments to be agreed at an IGC, there must be common accord (unanimous agreement) by the representatives of the Governments of the Member States. Once such agreement is reached, each Member State, in accordance with its respective constitutional requirements, must then ratify any new treaty. Once such ratification is obtained, the treaty may then come into effect on a pre-designated date.

II. SECONDARY SOURCES OF EC LAW

1. Secondary legislation

Article 249 EC provides that: '...the European Parliament acting jointly with the Council, the Council and the Commission shall make regulations and issue directives, take decisions, make recommendations and deliver opinions.'

From this Article, it is clear that three of the Community's institutions may be concerned with the creation of secondary legislation and that there are five forms that such legislation may take.

Community legislators (usually the Commission) are free to choose which form legislation is to take *unless* the Treaty otherwise prescribes. Each form of secondary legislation will be considered in turn.

i. Regulations

Article 249 EC provides that: 'A regulation shall have general application. It shall be binding in its entirety and directly applicable in all Member States.'

The fact that a regulation will have 'general application' and is 'binding in its entirety' simply means that a regulation will be effective throughout the Community, on every Member State and in full. Regulations must be published in the Official Journal and come into force on the date specified by the regulation or, if no such date is specified, on the twentieth day following publication.

The exact meaning of 'direct applicability' has been the cause of some debate, but it is now accepted that it denotes that regulations automatically take effect in each Member State without the need for national implementing measures. The ECJ has gone as far as to provide that Member States shall not pass any measure which professes to incorporate a Community regulation into national law (Case 34/73, *Variola*), as this could result in each Member State placing its own interpretation on the legislation.

Regulations achieve uniformity of law throughout the EC.

ii. Directives

Article 249 EC provides that: '.... directive shall be binding, as to the result to be achieved, upon each Member State to which it is addressed, but shall leave to the national authorities the choice of form and methods.'

Directives differ from regulations in a number of ways. They do not have general application and so do not have to be addressed to all Member States. Additionally, they are not directly applicable and, normally, the rights and obligations created by them only become effective once they have been incorporated into national law by the appropriate national authorities. They do, however, place an obligation on Member States to ensure that a particular aim is achieved by a particular date, leaving national authorities to decide on the implementation details. This allows a far greater degree of flexibility, providing Member States with the opportunity to introduce a measure in the manner best suited to that State.

Directives are often the chosen method where harmonisation, rather than uniformity, of law is the aim.

iii. Decisions

Article 249 EC provides that 'a decision shall be binding in its entirety upon those to whom it is addressed.'

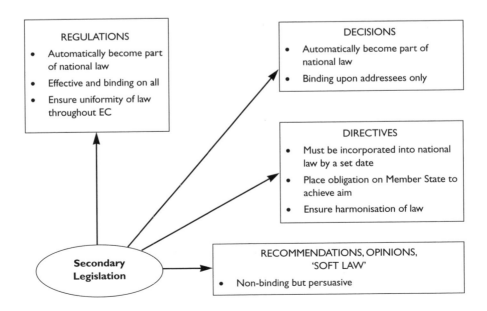

A decision is similar to a regulation in that it has direct applicability, requiring no national implementation in order to take effect. All decisions must be published in the Official Journal, taking effect on a prescribed date or on the twentieth day following publication.

It should be noted, however, that decisions are only binding on those to whom they are addressed. (Decisions may be addressed to individual Member States and both natural and legal persons.)

iv. Recommendations, Opinions and 'soft' law

Unlike regulations, directives and decisions, recommendations and opinions are not legally binding.

Article 249 EC provides that they have 'no binding force', although they are persuasive and should be taken into account by national courts (Case C-322/88, *Grimaldi*). Such sources of law are sometimes known as 'soft law'. Other sources of soft law may include guidelines or codes of conduct issued by the Community institutions.

2. Creating secondary legislation

All binding Community secondary legislation is subject to review by the ECJ, which may adjudicate on its validity. It is particularly important that the correct procedures are followed when creating such legislation, as failure to do so may render the legislation invalid. (Judicial review of legally enforceable acts of the institutions is discussed in Chapter 6.)

i. The legal base for the creation of secondary legislation

Community legislators must demonstrate that they have the necessary authority to enact secondary legislation. Article 253 EC provides that the preamble to regulations, directives and decisions should contain a statement as to the legal basis on which the legislation is made. Such authority will derive from a Treaty article empowering the institutions to legislate and is known as the 'legal base'.

The choice of legal base will depend on the subject matter of the proposed legislation. If, for example, the Community wishes to legislate on the free movement of workers, the Community's legal 'authority' for doing so is provided by Art 40 EC. Where no specific law making powers are provided, Art 308 EC may provide a general power to legislate in order to attain 'one of the objectives of the Community'.

It is vitally important that the correct legal base be used, as to do otherwise would allow legislation to be successfully challenged under the judicial review procedure (Chapter 6). An example of this can be found in Case C-376/98, *Germany v Parliament & Council ('Tobacco Advertising' case)* where Art 95, the legal base for measures relating to the functioning of the Internal Market, was used in order to enact Directive 98/43/EC, which imposed a general ban on tobacco advertising. The ECJ held that as the measure was not 'intended to improve the conditions for the establishment and functioning of the internal market' the incorrect legal base had been used and the directive was consequently declared void.

ii. Legislative procedures

The Community's legislative process is complicated, providing a number of different procedures by which secondary legislation may be enacted. It should be borne in mind that the issue of which procedure is to be followed in any one set of circumstances does not depend on the form that the legislation is to take, but on the procedure identified by the legal base. Thus, for example, if the Community wishes to enact legislation relating to the free movement of workers, the subject matter and therefore the legal base (Art 40 EC) will be the decisive feature, not the form that the legislation was to take – the procedure would not differ if a directive were drafted rather than a regulation.

Generally, the Commission is the initiator of draft legislation. This can be at its own instigation or following a request from the Council (Art 208 EC) or the Parliament (Art 192 EC).

In most circumstances, the Council will be the adopting institution. The primary distinguishing feature of each procedure is the degree of involvement that it provides to the EP, although it may also have an effect on which method of voting must be followed by the Council – that is, simple majority, unanimity or, more usually, qualified majority. (The implications of which voting procedure is applicable are discussed later in this chapter.)

An outline of the various procedures has already been provided in Chapter 3, but the following text will provide a recap.

iii. The Commission acting alone

This method is rarely used and it is sufficient to say that it involves the Commission acting without intervention from the other Community institutions (an example of the use of this procedure may be found under Art 86(3) EC).

The Commission also enjoys delegated legislative power. Although not strictly a legislative procedure, the Council may, through parent legislation, authorise the Commission to enact regulations in specific areas such as agriculture and competition; this allows legislation to be enacted quickly in areas that are highly regulated.

iv. The Council and Commission acting alone

Here the Council may adopt a proposal from the Commission without having to refer to any other authority (an example of this procedure may be found under Art 26 EC).

v. The 'Consultation' Procedure

Under this procedure, the Commission puts forward a draft proposal to the Council who, in turn, passes it to the EP for its opinion. No obligation is placed on either the Council or the Commission to follow such an opinion, but the resulting legislation may be annulled if the EP is not consulted (for example, Case 138/79, *Roquette Frères v Council*).

This procedure was provided by the original EEC Treaty and, therefore, before the EP became a directly elected body. It endows the EP with very little power, other than that of bringing the provision to the attention of others through debate. The Consultation Procedure is certainly no longer the 'norm' but is still used in a number of areas, an example of which can be found under Art 19 EC.

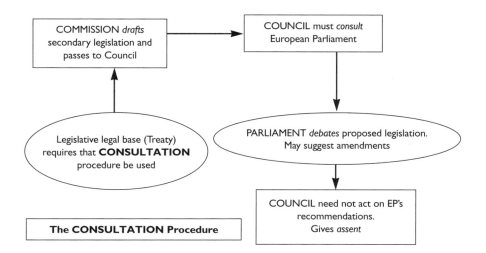

vi. The 'Co-operation' Procedure

The SEA established this procedure in order to provide the EP with greater legislative powers, following the introduction of direct elections.

The procedure, which is contained within Art 252 EC, provides that the Council, following a proposal from the Commission, and on which it has obtained the EP's opinion, will adopt a 'common position' which, in turn, is communicated to the EP. The EP then has a number of avenues open to it. It may:

(a) approve the common position – in which case, the Council may adopt the proposal by qualified majority;

(b) fail to reply within three months – in which case, once more, the Council may adopt the provision as above;

(c) reject common position OR propose amendments – in which case, the Council may overrule the EP but only if the Council acts unanimously.

If unanimity is not possible, the Commission will be required to re-submit, within one month, the draft legislation after taking into account the EP's amendments. The Council may then adopt the proposal, normally within three months.

While this procedure clearly provides the EP with more legislative power than it enjoyed previously, it does not give the Parliament the power

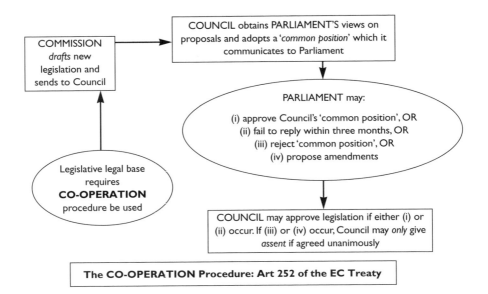

The CO-OPERATION Procedure: Art 252 of the EC Treaty

to enact or veto legislation. It was, however, considered to be a major innovation in the Community system requiring both the Council and Commission to take far more cognisance of the Parliament's opinions.

Since its introduction, the Community has continued to enhance the legislative powers of the EP via other legislative procedures and, as a result, the range of application of the co-operation procedure has significantly diminished.

vii. The 'Co-decision' Procedure

Introduced by the TEU, provided by Art 251 EC, this further enhances the powers of the EP. Now modified by the ToA, the complex procedure initially involves the Commission sending a legislative proposal to both the Council and the EP. At this stage, providing agreement can be reached, the Council may adopt the legislation by qualified majority.

Should consensus not be reached, the Council may adopt a 'common position', which must be communicated to the EP. The EP has three months to approve the Council's common position. If approved, the legislation may be adopted. (Failure to reply within three months will have the same effect.) If, on the other hand, the EP rejects, by absolute majority, the Council's common position, the proposed act will be deemed to have failed.

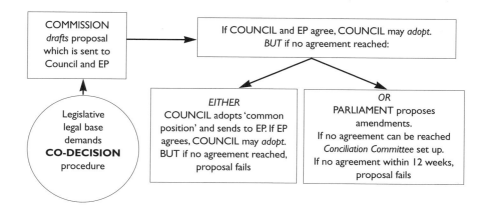

The CO-DECISION Procedure: Art 251 of the EC Treaty

Alternatively, the EP may wish to propose amendments. Provided it does so after agreeing by absolute majority, such amendments should be sent to the Council and the Commission. Should the Council agree to the amendments within three months, the provision may be adopted by unanimity.

If agreement cannot be reached, a Conciliation Committee is set up, comprising representatives of both the Council and the EP and involving the Commission, in an attempt to reach consensus. There is then a period of 12 weeks in which to agree and adopt the proposed legislation. It is possible that this period may be extended but if the text is not approved within the time limit set, it will be deemed not to have been adopted.

This procedure provides the EP with considerable legislative power, as the Parliament may actually veto proposed legislation. This is particularly noteworthy, bearing in mind that each institution represents different, but equally important interests and goes some way in establishing the EP's position within the institutional balance of the Community.

viii. The 'Assent' Procedure

In a small number of areas, the positive approval of the EP is required before the Council can adopt a proposal. This procedure, introduced by the SEA, affords the EP with an absolute power of rejection. An example of its use can be found under Art 161 EC.

3. Legislative processes – how decisions are reached

While it is important to get to grips with the variety of legislative procedures by which the Community may enact secondary legislation, there is far more to the legislative process than mere procedure.

i. The 'institutional balance'

The original Treaty split power between the Council and the Commission and so, at the time, it was necessary to ensure the correct balance was reached between the federal tendencies of the Commission and the intergovernmental nature of the Council. The need to ensure balance within the Community has since been complicated by the introduction of direct elections to the Parliament, which has consequently demanded, and received, far greater involvement in the legislative process.

As each of these institutions represent different interests (the Council represents the interests of the Member States governments, the Parliament, the citizens and the Commission, the Community as a whole), the legislative processes have to ensure that all such interests are appropriately balanced.

Interinstitutional co-operation

As legislative procedures have developed, there has been a far greater need to ensure interinstitutional co-operation, both in the planning of legislative strategies and with regard to the content of legislative acts. With regard to the former, an interinstitutional co-ordination group (known as the Neuneither Group, after its founder) has, for example, been set up to plan future legislative programmes and the Commission consults widely with interested parties before putting forward legislative proposals.

Such consultation allows the interests of the Member States, citizens, the Community as a whole and a variety of pressure groups to be taken into consideration.

In addition to co-operation between the institutions with regard to the formulation of legislative policies, with the increased use of the co-decision procedure in particular, there is also a need for interinstitutional co-operation in order to ensure policies become Acts.

Once the Commission has formulated draft legislation, it will be sent to the Parliament and/or the Council (depending on the procedure to be followed), which will consider the proposal, usually via a number of working groups or committees.

At this stage, there may be conflict between Member States within the Council or between political groups within the Parliament, and agreement will have to be reached within the institutions by means of negotiation and compromise. Once the Council and the Parliament have agreed their individual positions with regard to a legislative proposal, if their opinions diverge, it will often be left to the Commission to broker agreement between the two if the legislative proposal is to succeed.

While the above discussion is, of necessity, brief, it hopefully provides some food for thought as to the democratic nature of the decision-making processes within the Community. While the question of who runs Europe was considered in Chapter 3, it is suggested that issues are far more complex than they may first appear. Not only do the competing interests of the Community institutions have to be balanced, but also the competing interests of the various groups within the institutions, such as the various Member States, political parties and so on.

III. CASE LAW OF THE ECJ

The Court's function, as provided by Art 220 EC, is to 'ensure that in the interpretation and application of this Treaty the law is observed'. As the Treaties and secondary legislation are often imprecise or insufficiently comprehensive, this has provided the ECJ with the opportunity to significantly contribute to the corpus of Community law.

The importance of the Court's case law should not be underestimated. By virtue of its favoured purposive method of interpretation (use your Glossary!) – and its jurisdiction to provide preliminary rulings (discussed in Chapter 6) – the Court has developed the Community's legal system, constitutionalising the Treaties and filling in gaps in the law. While there is no formal system of precedent and the Court is free to depart from its own past decisions, in the interest of consistency, this seldom occurs. With regard to the relationship between the ECJ's decisions and national courts, the ECJ's decisions do have a precedential value, as can be evidenced by the Court's dicta in Cases 28–30/62, *Da Costa* (discussed further in Chapter 6).

The case of *Van Gend en Loos* (Case 26/62) epitomises the importance of the case law of the EC, demonstrating the Court's approach to its role and also its impact. It is consequently strongly recommended that students read this judgement and consider its consequences. (The case is discussed in further detail in Chapter 5.)

IV. GENERAL PRINCIPLES OF COMMUNITY LAW

General principles of law, which can be found in all advanced legal systems, have the function of assisting where written sources of law are not sufficiently comprehensive. The general principles of Community law have been developed by the ECJ and have been used to 'flesh out' the law found in the Treaties and secondary legislation.

General principles of Community law have been held to include the following:

- equality
- fundamental rights
- proportionality
- subsidiarity
- legal certainty.

1. The function and status of general principles

General principles have been used by the ECJ to assist it in the interpretation of Community legislation and also as a factor when considering the validity of secondary legislation (Case 112/77, *Topfer v Commission*). In addition, they provide a restraint on the activities of the Member States (Case 11/70, *Internationale Handelsgesellschaft*, where the Court provided that a public authority must recognise the principle of proportionality in its dealings with citizens.)

The ECJ has been creative in developing these principles, using the purposive method of interpretation and discovering them in:

- the Treaties themselves;
- the legal systems of the Member States; and
- international law.

The ECJ has justified its actions by referring to three Treaty Articles which, it argues, gives it the necessary authority, namely:

- Art 220 EC, which provides that 'The Court of Justice shall ensure that in the interpretation of the Treaty the law is observed,' the term 'law' in this context being understood to mean more than the written sources of law contained in the Treaties;

- Art 230 EC, which provides 'infringement of this Treaty or any rule of law relating to its application'. 'Any rule of law' in this context has been interpreted to be a reference to law other than that contained in the Treaty;

- Art 288 EC, which refers to 'general principles common to the laws of the Member States'.

In order to provide a flavour of how these principles have been developed and applied, a number of examples will be considered in turn.

2. Equality – 'discovered' in the Treaties

The Treaty refers to the principle of equality on a number of occasions and is an example of the Court developing a general principle by bringing together 'threads' found in the Treaty.

While Art 12 EC prohibits discrimination on the grounds of nationality, Art 34(2) EC prohibits discrimination between producers or consumers within the Community. In addition, Art 141 EC provides for equal pay between men and women, and the Court, on the basis of these 'threads', has developed a far more general principle of non-discrimination.

The Court has gone on to use the principle to prohibit discrimination based on grounds such as nationality (Case 293/83, *Gravier v City of Liège*) and gender (Cases 75a and 117/82, *Razzouk and Beydouin v Commission*).

The principle of equality or non-discrimination would now appear to be formally supported by the Treaty as the ToA introduced Art 13 EC, which provides the Community with the authority to legislate in order to prohibit discrimination based on 'sex, racial or ethnic origin, religion or belief, disability, age or sexual orientation'.

3. Fundamental Rights – 'discovered' in national and international law

Although not originally mentioned in the (largely economic) Treaties, the ECJ, in cases such as Case 29/69, *Stauder v City of Ulm* and Case 11/70, *Internationale Handelsgesellschaft*, has confirmed that rights guaranteed under German national law are also to be protected by the Community. Similarly, the ECJ, in Case 36/75, *Rutili v Ministre de l'Interieur*, confirmed that rights found in the European Convention for the Protection of Human Rights and Fundamental Freedoms (ECHR) would be protected by the Court.

Once again the proactive approach of the Court appears to have been vindicated. The ToA amended the TEU (Art 6 TEU) which now declares that the EU 'shall respect fundamental rights', while a Charter of Fundamental Rights has also been drawn up. The legal status of this Charter is still under debate but at present it has persuasive rather than binding effect.

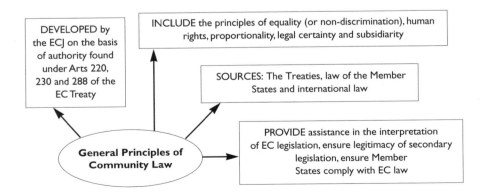

DEVELOPED by the ECJ on the basis of authority found under Arts 220, 230 and 288 of the EC Treaty

INCLUDE the principles of equality (or non-discrimination), human rights, proportionality, legal certainty and subsidiarity

SOURCES: The Treaties, law of the Member States and international law

General Principles of Community Law

PROVIDE assistance in the interpretation of EC legislation, ensure legitimacy of secondary legislation, ensure Member States comply with EC law

V. INTERNATIONAL AGREEMENTS

The EC has legal personality (Art 281 EC) and is empowered (by Art 300 EC) to enter into international agreements which are an integral source of Community law.

The Commission has been provided with the role of negotiator of international agreements. Following authorisation by the Council, the Commission conducts negotiations, assisted by various committees. The ECJ may be required to consider the legality of any agreement, which will be put before the Council of the European Union in the same manner as draft legislation. The Council may then give its assent to the agreement, after involving the EP as appropriate to the field in which the agreement is being concluded (Art 300 EC). Such agreements are binding on both the Community and on the Member States.

VI. CONCLUSIONS

Community law is an evolving legal system, containing rules that provide rights, obligations and remedies. It has evolved over time and continues to develop in response to the needs and objectives of Europe. Contained in numerous sources, it is made up of rules which effectively provide the Community's constitution, direction on how the Community is to be administered and also the substantive law of the Community. Once this has been understood, the time is right to consider the relationship that exists between Community law and the law of the Member States.

5 The Relationship between Community Law and the National Legal Systems of the Member States

I. THE DOCTRINES OF DIRECT EFFECT AND SUPREMACY

The status of EC law within the legal systems of the various Member States is of fundamental importance and there are a number of questions that must be answered before an understanding of Community law and its impact can be fully gained.

First, it is necessary to consider the *effect* of EC law in the Member States, who receives *rights* and *obligations* under it and whether and where such rights may be *enforced*. Second, it is necessary to consider which source of law will take precedence should there be a conflict between EC law and national law.

1. The original position

Surprisingly, the founding Treaties did not address these questions directly and the original Member States assumed that EC law would have the same domestic effects as international law, resulting in the status of the EC Treaty being determined by each Member State's own constitutional rules.

In dualist States (such as the United Kingdom), international law is only binding on national courts if it has been adopted by the national authorities and made part of domestic law. In such States, it was therefore considered that the EC Treaty would not provide enforceable rights to citizens unless specifically incorporated.

On the other hand, in monist States (such as the Netherlands), once ratified, international law automatically forms part of the national legal system. In Member States with such a constitution, it was consequently assumed that EC law automatically became part of that State's domestic legal system. As a result, the status – and impact – of EC law varied from state to state.

The ECJ has, however, taken a different approach to the question of the impact of Community law and has developed two principles, which have become known as the 'Twin Pillars' upon which the Community rests, namely, direct effect and supremacy. Each will be considered in turn.

II. THE DOCTRINE OF DIRECT EFFECT OF EC LAW

1. The creation of the doctrine

The ECJ provided a ground-breaking judgement in Case 26/62, *Van Gend en Loos* (*Van Gend*). *Van Gend* had imported a quantity of chemicals from Germany into the Netherlands and was required, by Dutch law, to pay customs duty to the Dutch authorities. The importers challenged the legality of the duty, claiming that it was an infringement of Art 12 EC (now Art 25). The Dutch tribunal referred the question to the ECJ under the preliminary reference procedure (Art 234 EC, Chapter 6).

In order to arrive at its decision, the ECJ drew heavily on its purposive method of interpretation (look at the Glossary), relying not only on the wording of the Treaties, but also on the spirit and aims of the Community. In its judgement, the ECJ declared that 'the Community constitutes a new legal order of international law' which confers both rights and obligations on individuals, as well as on the participating Member States, without the need for implementing legislation. The Court further concluded that

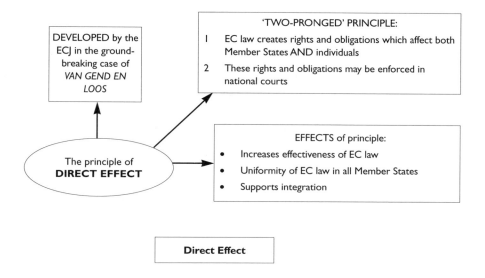

Direct Effect

national courts must protect such rights. In other words, the ECJ provided that EC law has direct effect, which can be seen as a two-pronged concept under which:

- Community law provides not only Member States with rights and obligations, but individuals also; and
- such rights and obligations can be enforced by individuals before their national courts.

From this judgement, which was opposed by a number of Member States including the Netherlands and Belgium, it can be concluded that the Court was motivated by the need to ensure the integration, effectiveness and uniformity of Community law.

2. The conditions for direct effect

The ECJ explained in *Van Gend* that not all Treaty articles would be capable of direct effect and it is now clear that any provision must first fulfil a set of criteria if it is to have direct effect (these criteria will hereafter be called the *Van Gend* criteria, for ease of explanation. It should be noted that some sources may refer to the *'Reyners* criteria' after the case in which they were first listed together). The *Van Gend* criteria require that in order to have direct effect, the legal provision must be as follows.

i. Clear and precise

It is logical that if law is to be enforceable, both parties must be clear as to what their respective rights/obligations are. The ECJ has therefore declared that a provision must be 'sufficiently clear and precise' before being capable of direct effect. This does not necessarily mean that the whole provision must comply: in Case 43/75, *Defrenne v Sabena*, for example, it was held that only part of Art 119 EC (now Art 141) fulfilled this criteria but was consequently directly effective.

ii. Unconditional

A provision will not be unconditional if the right it provides is in some way dependent on the judgement or discretion of an independent body unless that discretion is subject to judicial control (an example of this may be found in Case 41/74, *Van Duyn*).

iii. Not subject to any further implementing measures on the part of either the Community or national authority

This criterion would appear to have been subject to rather liberal application by the ECJ, as can be demonstrated in Case 2/74, *Reyners v Belgium*. In this case, based on the wording of the Treaty, it had been anticipated that the Community would have to enact secondary legislation before the objectives contained in Art 52 EC (now Art 43) would provide rights to individuals. However, the Court declared the provision to be directly effective, explaining that to do otherwise could result in individuals being denied their Community law rights.

3. Direct effect of the various sources of Community law

The doctrine of direct effect has been further developed and expanded upon over the years and the important developments are set out below.

i. Direct effect and Treaty articles

As we have already seen above, the question of whether the principle of direct effect applies to Treaty articles was considered in the judgement of *Van Gend en Loos* when Art 12 EC (now Art 25) was held to be directly effective. It is now accepted that Treaty articles are capable of direct effect, *providing* that they comply with the three *Van Gend* criteria.

In addition, the Court has provided that rights and obligations contained in Treaty articles may be enforced both against the State and public bodies (*vertical* direct effect) and against private bodies and individuals (*horizontal* direct effect: Case 43/75, *Defrenne v Sabena*).

ii. Direct effect and regulations

Article 249 EC would appear to give regulations direct effect, providing as it does that a regulation 'shall be binding in its entirety and directly applicable in all Member States'. Direct applicability should be interpreted as meaning that a provision requires no implementation or further action by the Member States in order for it to take effect in national law. While all regulations (*and* Treaty articles) are directly applicable, the Court confirmed in Case 9/70, *Franz Grad*, that regulations would be directly effective only when able to fulfil ALL of the *Van Gend* criteria. As with Treaty articles, regulations may be enforced both vertically and horizontally.

iii. Direct effect and decisions

Decisions, as regulations, are directly applicable, but Art 249 EC provides that they can be binding only on those to whom they are addressed (whether that be Member States, corporations or individuals). The ECJ has held that decisions will be directly effective, providing they fulfil the *Van Gend* criteria, but only against an addressee (Case 9/70, *Franz Grad*).

iv. Direct effect of international agreements

This is a controversial and complex area, outside the scope of this book. It is sufficient to conclude that in an attempt to ensure that Member States respect any commitments arising from agreements concluded with non-Member States, the ECJ has ruled that such agreements may have direct effect if the circumstances are appropriate (Case 104/81, *Kupferberg*).

v. Direct effect and directives

This has proved to be a particularly controversial area.

Article 249 EC provides that: 'A directive shall be binding, as to the result to be achieved, upon each Member State to which it is addressed, but shall leave to the national authorities the choice of form and methods.' Directives are therefore *not* directly applicable, as they require implementation into national law by a State's legislative body. Consequently, directives do not appear to provide rights to individuals until they are incorporated – and then via national legislation, rather than the directive itself – although they do place obligations on Member States.

Despite the wording of Art 249, which would appear to preclude directives from being directly effective, the ECJ has held that where a directive has not been properly implemented into national law, it may still give rise to direct effects (*Franz Grad* and *Van Duyn*).

The Court has confirmed that in order for directives to be directly effective, they must satisfy the *Van Gend* criteria. While the first two criteria present few problems, it would appear that the final criterion is impossible to satisfy. However, once the date on which the directive *should* have been implemented has passed, the ECJ has shown itself willing to conclude that this criterion has also been satisfied (Case 148/78, *Pubblico Ministero v Ratti*).

The Court has argued that this approach makes directives both more effective and also stops Member States from relying on their own 'wrongdoing', should they fail to incorporate a directive into domestic law. This development has not been without its critics, however, who argue that to allow directives to be directly effective removes the distinction between regulations and directives.

In response to such criticism, the ECJ has explained that directives are distinct as they may only be enforced vertically (that is, against the State) and not horizontally (that is, against individuals) (Case 152/84, *Marshall v Southampton and South West Hampshire AHA* (*Marshall* (*No 1*)).

In the *Marshall* case, Miss Marshall wished to enforce rights emanating from the Equal Treatment Directive (Council Directive (76/207/EEC)) against her employer. She attempted to do this in the appropriate national court – an employment tribunal (ET). The ET made a preliminary reference to the ECJ (under Art 234 EC), asking whether she could rely on the directive. The Court replied that she could do so, as she wished to rely on the provisions of the directive against the State, who were one and the same as her employers. In other words, she could rely on the vertical direct effect of the directive.

This requirement has the unfortunate effect of discriminating between individuals who wish to enforce their rights against the State, as compared to those wishing to pursue the same rights against an individual. The problem can be illustrated by consideration of Case 151/84, *Roberts v Tate & Lyle Industries* (the *Tate & Lyle* case), which mirrored the circumstances of *Marshall* (*No 1*). Ms Roberts also wished to enforce rights emanating from the Equal Treatment Directive but, as she was employed by a private corporation as opposed to an emanation of the State, her rights were unenforceable. The ECJ has attempted to mitigate such discriminatory effects by providing a wide interpretation of 'State', as can be seen below.

III. DEVELOPING THE EFFECTIVENESS OF COMMUNITY LAW

1. What bodies are considered to be part of the State?

In an attempt to circumnavigate the problems highlighted above, the ECJ has shown itself to be willing to adopt the widest possible definition of 'State'.

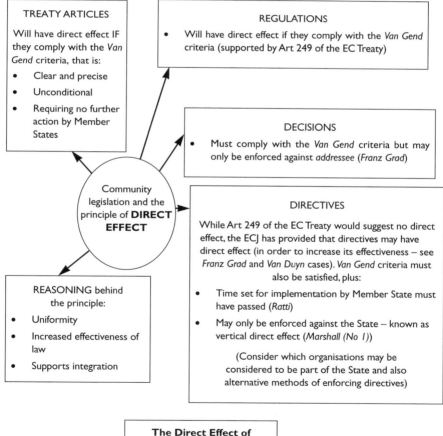

TREATY ARTICLES

Will have direct effect IF they comply with the *Van Gend* criteria, that is:

- Clear and precise
- Unconditional
- Requiring no further action by Member States

REGULATIONS

- Will have direct effect if they comply with the *Van Gend* criteria (supported by Art 249 of the EC Treaty)

DECISIONS

- Must comply with the *Van Gend* criteria but may only be enforced against *addressee* (*Franz Grad*)

Community legislation and the principle of **DIRECT EFFECT**

DIRECTIVES

While Art 249 of the EC Treaty would suggest no direct effect, the ECJ has provided that directives may have direct effect (in order to increase its effectiveness – see *Franz Grad* and *Van Duyn* cases). *Van Gend* criteria must also be satisfied, plus:

- Time set for implementation by Member State must have passed (*Ratti*)
- May only be enforced against the State – known as vertical direct effect (*Marshall (No 1)*)

(Consider which organisations may be considered to be part of the State and also alternative methods of enforcing directives)

REASONING behind the principle:

- Uniformity
- Increased effectiveness of law
- Supports integration

The Direct Effect of Community Legislation

69

As already discussed, the ECJ has been willing to recognise an Area Health Authority as part of the State, while in Case 103/88, *Fratelli Constanzo*, regional and local government were also considered to be within the definition. In Case 222/84, *Johnston v Chief Constable of the RUC*, the Chief Constable was also recognised as being an 'emanation of the State'.

In Case C-188/89, *Foster v British Gas*, the ECJ provided some guidance by explaining that a directive may be relied upon against organisations or bodies which:

• have been made responsible for providing a public service, which may be subject to the authority or control of the State, and/or
• has special powers beyond those which result from the normal rules applicable to relations between individuals.

These guidelines, while failing to provide an inclusive definition of 'State', have nevertheless proved helpful by making it clear that something *more* than mere control is necessary.

This conclusion is supported by the Court of Appeal's dicta in *Doughty v Rolls Royce* (1992). Although Rolls Royce was, at the time of the action, wholly owned by the State, it was not considered an emanation of the State, as the company neither provided a public service nor had any of the 'special powers' referred to in *Foster*.

2. Indirect effect

The ECJ's refusal to allow the horizontal direct effect of directives has without doubt lessened their effectiveness. In an attempt at remedying this, the Court has developed a principle, which has become known as indirect effect or 'the interpretative obligation'.

i. The basic principle

In Case 14/83, *Von Colson*, the ECJ reminded Member States of their duty under Art 10 EC (then Art 5) 'to ensure the fulfilment of the obligations...resulting from action taken by the institutions of the Community'. The Court went on to explain that such obligations also bind all the authorities of the States 'including, for matters within their jurisdiction, the courts'. Consequently, an obligation is placed on national courts to interpret and apply national law in a manner, which is consistent with the wording and purpose of directives.

This judgement has been the subject of much academic criticism as it requires national courts to supplement the role of the domestic legislator.

The principle has also been criticised for allowing the direct effect of directives via the 'back door', without the need to ensure that the restrictive *Van Gend* criteria can be fulfilled.

The principle has, however, undoubtedly succeeded in enhancing the effectiveness of unimplemented and incorrectly implemented directives, while at the same time placing another obstacle in the path of Member States who may fail to comply with their obligations.

ii. The development of the doctrine of indirect effect

The *Von Colson* judgement left a number of questions unanswered with regard to the exact extent of the principle of 'indirect effect'.

In Case 80/86, *Kolpinghuis Nijmegen*, the Court made it clear that it would not be possible to interpret national legislation in the light of a directive should this result in conflict with any of the general principles of Community law, such as non-retroactivity or legitimate expectation (Chapter 4 provides consideration of general principles). Thus, it is clear that there are limits on the application of indirect effect and national courts need only interpret national law to conform with Community Directives 'in so far as it is possible'.

In Case C-106/89, *Marleasing*, the ECJ confirmed that national legislation which has been interpreted by a national court in the light of a non-implemented or incorrectly implemented directive can be relied on, not only by an individual against the State, but also against another individual and even where such national law had been enacted prior to the directive and was not intended to implement it. This would appear to be allowing unincorporated directives to be enforced against individuals, thus achieving 'horizontal direct effect' in all but name. However, it appears that the decision in *Marleasing* has been tempered in Case C-456/98, *Centrosteel*, where the ECJ provided that a directive cannot of itself impose obligations on individuals in the absence of proper implementing legislation, in particular those relating to criminal liability, although it may impose civil liability or obligations that may not otherwise have existed.

Academics have highlighted that indirect effect is the *most used* means of ensuring proper effect of incorrectly or unimplemented directives and its importance should not, consequently, be underestimated. The ECJ has regularly reaffirmed its importance and in joined Cases C-397-403/01 *Pfeiffer and Others* (a case relating to the 'Working Time Directive'), provided that '*the requirement for national law to be interpreted in conformity with Community law is inherent in the system of the Treaty ... to ensure the full effectiveness of Community law ... '.*

3. 'Triangular' or 'incidental' direct effect

Despite the ECJ's decision in *Marshall* (*No 1*) prohibiting the horizontal direct effect of directives, decisions such as Case C-194/94, *CIA Security International* appear to provide limited horizontal effects, providing that no legal obligations are directly imposed on individuals. It would appear that where an individual invokes a directive against another private party, in an attempt to demonstrate the illegality of national legislation, and this adversely affects the third party, this will be accepted by the ECJ despite the fact that it equates with horizontal direct effect of the directive. Once more, the ECJ has cited the enhanced effectiveness of directives as its aim.

It has to be stressed, however, that the case law in this area to date is both limited and contradictory and the extent of the principle is, as yet, rather uncertain.

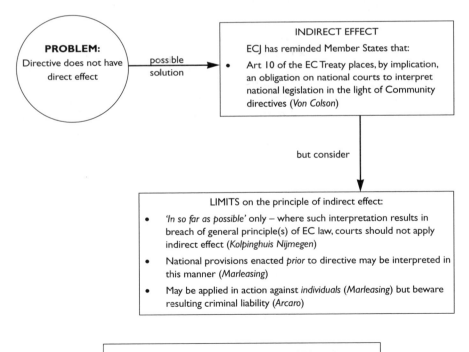

PROBLEM:
Directive does not have direct effect

possible solution

INDIRECT EFFECT
ECJ has reminded Member States that:
- Art 10 of the EC Treaty places, by implication, an obligation on national courts to interpret national legislation in the light of Community directives (*Von Colson*)

but consider

LIMITS on the principle of indirect effect:
- *'In so far as possible'* only – where such interpretation results in breach of general principle(s) of EC law, courts should not apply indirect effect (*Kolpinghuis Nijmegen*)
- National provisions enacted *prior* to directive may be interpreted in this manner (*Marleasing*)
- May be applied in action against *individuals* (*Marleasing*) but beware resulting criminal liability (*Arcaro*)

The Doctrine of Indirect Effect of Directives

4. State liability for damages (*Francovich* damages)

In view of the limitations placed on the direct effect of directives and despite the possibility of enforcing rights under the principle of indirect effect, a number of barriers may still exist with regard to the enforcement of rights emanating from a directive (there may, for example, be no national law to interpret or interpretation may simply not be possible).

In Cases C-6 and 9/90, *Francovich and Bonifaci v Italy* (*Francovich*), the ECJ held that, should a Member State fail to incorporate a directive into national law, an individual who suffers damage as a consequence may claim compensation from the State, thereby ensuring greater effectiveness of directives.

This right to compensation was, however, subject to a number of criteria, namely:

1 the directive must confer a right on citizens;
2 the content of the right must be identifiable by reference to the directive;
3 there must be a causal link between the State's breach and the individual's damage.

The Court's judgement in *Francovich* reinforces the Member States' obligations under Art 10 EC and also provides a further incentive to Member States to ensure that EC law rights are not denied to citizens.

This ruling has been of immense importance to Community law and the principle has been clarified and extended in a number of later cases, particularly Cases C-46 and C-48/93, *Brasserie du Pêcheur SA v Germany*; *R v Secretary of State for Transport ex p Factortame Ltd and Others* (*Pêcheur and Factortame*).

i. The development of State damages

In *Francovich*, the ECJ's decision related to a Member State's failure to fulfil its obligations in relation to directives but, in *Pêcheur* and *Factortame*, the ECJ confirmed that damages could also be available in situations where a Member State had failed to observe other sources of Community law. Once more, however, the Court explained that certain criteria must be fulfilled:

- the rule of law infringed must be intended to confer rights on individuals;
- the breach must be sufficiently serious;
- there must be a direct causal link between the breach and the damage caused.

The Court also provided that the principle applied to whichever organ of the State was responsible for the breach or omission, whether it be legislative, executive or, controversially, judicial (as in Case C-224/01 *Kobler v Austria*).

ii. The ECJ's interpretation of 'sufficiently serious'

With regard to what will constitute a 'sufficiently serious' breach, the Court has put forward various factors which may be taken into account, including the following:

- the degree of clarity and precision of the EC rule that has been breached (if the rule is imprecisely worded, the breach will not be sufficiently serious: Case C-392/93, *R v HM Treasury ex p British Telecom*);

- the 'intentionality' or 'voluntariness' of the infringement and the damage caused (intentional fault is not essential: Cases T-178, 179 and 188–90/94, *Dillenkofer v Germany*);

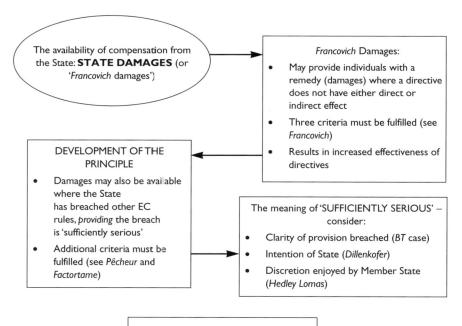

- the degree of discretion provided to the Member State by the provision (where there is no, or limited, discretion, the infringement of law in itself may be sufficient to establish the existence of a sufficiently serious breach: Case C-5/94, *R v MAFF ex p Hedley Lomas*).

By allowing individuals to bring such actions before their national courts, it should be quite clear that the ECJ has once more enhanced the effectiveness of Community law.

IV. THE DOCTRINE OF SUPREMACY OF COMMUNITY LAW

EC Member States have two legal systems with which to contend – that of their own national law and that of the EC. It therefore needs to be considered how the Member States are required to react should these sources of law conflict. Once more, the Treaty is largely silent and it has been left to the ECJ to provide guidance.

i. The creation of the doctrine

While the ECJ did not address the issue of supremacy of Community law directly in its *Van Gend en Loos* judgement, it did provide that Community law constitutes a 'new legal order... for the benefit of which the States have limited their sovereign rights, albeit within limited fields'.

It is clear from the Court's dicta that it was recognised that to allow Member States to apply conflicting national law rather than Community law would severely undermine the ability of the Community to achieve its aims. Thus, the doctrine of the supremacy (or primacy) of Community law was first (tentatively) established.

ii. The development of the doctrine of supremacy

The precise implications of the doctrine of supremacy were not addressed until Case 6/64, *Costa v ENEL*. In its decision, the ECJ confirmed that where national law and EC law conflict, EC law must take precedence, even where the national law has been enacted subsequent to EC law, thus ruling out the possibility of national law taking precedence under the concept of 'implied repeal' (that is, a process recognised under UK law whereby later law will always be presumed to have automatically repealed any conflicting earlier enacted law).

The Court provided a number of arguments in support of its dicta. First, it confirmed that EC law is an integral part of domestic legal systems, also providing that Member States had created this new legal system by limiting their sovereign rights and transferring power to the Community.

Drawing heavily on the spirit and aims of the Treaty, the Court pointed out that the uniformity and effectiveness of Community law would be jeopardised should national law be allowed to take precedence. In addition, the Court argued that the obligations undertaken by the Member States would be 'merely contingent', rather than 'unconditional' if they could 'be called into question by subsequent [national] legal acts'.

The Court also referred directly to the text of the EC Treaty to support its judgement. Although the Treaty does not provide directly for the supremacy of Community law, the ECJ argued that Art 249 (then Art 189), which provides for the direct applicability of regulations, would be meaningless if Member States could negate their effect by enacting subsequent, conflicting legislation.

While *Van Gend* and *Costa* dealt with the theoretical principle of supremacy, the Court had little to say on the practical application of the concept. A serious threat to the supremacy of EC law was revealed in Case 11/70, *Internationale Handelsgesellschaft*, when the German Administrative Court voiced its concern over the legal foundations on which the principle of supremacy was based. The German Court's disquiet revolved around its concern that fundamental rights contained within the German constitution could be overruled by Community law. The ECJ made it clear that EC law is supreme over all forms and sources of national law, softening the blow by declaring that the Community recognised such fundamental rights as an 'integral part of the general principles of law' whose protection would be ensured 'within the structure and objectives of the Community'.

In Case 106/77, *Amministrazione delle Finanze dello Stato v Simmenthal*, as a result of a preliminary reference, the ECJ was required to consider whether a national court should disapply conflicting national legislation, even in situations where that court had no domestic jurisdiction to do so (in Italy, this function was carried out by the Constitutional Court). The ECJ provided that where conflict arises between national and Community law, the national court, under Community law, is required to give immediate effect to EC law and not wait for a ruling from the Constitutional Court.

This judgement is important, in that it confers on domestic courts jurisdiction that they may not have under domestic law. Once more, the ECJ emphasised the need for such action in order to ensure the effectiveness of Community law.

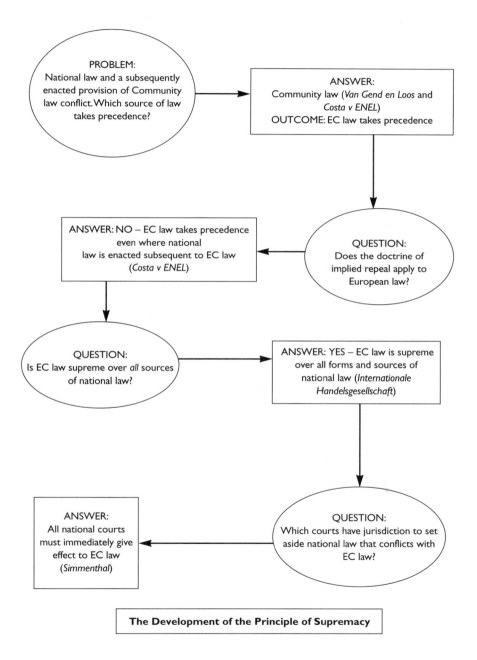

PROBLEM:
National law and a subsequently enacted provision of Community law conflict. Which source of law takes precedence?

ANSWER:
Community law (*Van Gend en Loos* and *Costa v ENEL*)
OUTCOME: EC law takes precedence

QUESTION:
Does the doctrine of implied repeal apply to European law?

ANSWER: NO – EC law takes precedence even where national law is enacted subsequent to EC law (*Costa v ENEL*)

QUESTION:
Is EC law supreme over *all* sources of national law?

ANSWER: YES – EC law is supreme over all forms and sources of national law (*Internationale Handelsgesellschaft*)

QUESTION:
Which courts have jurisdiction to set aside national law that conflicts with EC law?

ANSWER:
All national courts must immediately give effect to EC law (*Simmenthal*)

The Development of the Principle of Supremacy

A further example of the jurisdiction of national courts being extended by Community law can be found in Case C-213/89, *R v Secretary of State for Transport ex p Factortame Ltd* (*Factortame* (*No 2*)). In this case, the ECJ explained that a national rule must be set aside by the national court if that rule prevents the court from granting interim relief. This can be seen as an additional example of the practical consequences of the doctrine of supremacy.

V. CONCLUSIONS

Membership of the EC has resulted in the Member States having an additional source of law to contend with – that of the EC. Rather surprisingly, the Treaties give little guidance as to the interaction between national and Community law and it has been left to the ECJ to interpret which source of law is supreme in situations of conflict and also what effects EC law may have within the Member States.

The ECJ has reached the conclusion that EC law is not like other sources of international law. Not only is EC law supreme; it also provides rights and obligations to Member States and individuals alike which can, in turn, be enforced before national courts.

While these principles may appear simplistic and obvious, their effect on the EC has been profound, elevating its relevance and ensuring its uniform effectiveness throughout Europe.

6 Enforcing Community Law

In the preceding chapters, we have considered why the EC was created and how it has developed. We have also considered who 'runs' the Community and the various sources of law that make up the Community's legal system. In Chapter 5, we also considered the relationship between national and Community law. In order to understand how the Community works in practice, we now need to consider how EC law is enforced.

Because Community law forms part of each Member State's domestic legal system, rights and obligations emanating from European law are normally enforced before domestic courts rather than before the ECJ. This is quite logical, if it is remembered that EU law should be viewed as 'just another source' of national law. We therefore need to consider exactly on what basis and how such enforcement takes place.

National courts are not left totally to their own devices when applying EC law and so we will also consider the procedure known as 'preliminary reference' (Art 234 EC) which provides a valuable link between the ECJ and domestic courts.

While domestic courts are normally used to enforce EC law rights, there are certain actions that only the ECJ (or CFI) has jurisdiction to hear. These include 'infringement proceedings' against Member States who have failed to comply with their Community obligations (Arts 226–28 EC) and 'judicial review' of the acts and/or omissions of the Community institutions (including Arts 230–33 EC). Each will be considered in turn.

I. ENFORCING COMMUNITY LAW RIGHTS BEFORE NATIONAL COURTS

As has already been considered in Chapter 5, provided certain criteria are fulfilled, Community law has direct effect, that is, it provides individuals with rights and obligations that are enforceable before national courts. We therefore need to consider which domestic courts may be employed, what procedures should be followed and what remedies should be available to individuals enforcing their EC law rights.

1. Courts

It has been left to the Member States' discretion to decide which national courts will be appropriate to hear actions founded on Community law and also the procedures to be followed. In the United Kingdom, for example, an action relating to EC employment law would be heard before an Employment Tribunal.

As the ECJ stated in Case 45/76, *Comet BV v Produktschap voor Siergewassen* (*Comet*):

It is for the domestic law of each Member State to designate the courts having jurisdiction and the procedural conditions governing actions at law intended to ensure the protection of the rights which subjects derive from the direct effects of Community law.

2. Procedures

The dicta in *Comet* demonstrates that the enforcement of EC law rights in national courts has to fit in with the national systems already in place for enforcement of national law.

Harmonisation of procedures throughout the EC is not practicable due to the wide variety of approaches employed throughout the various Member States. Instead, in recognition of the Community's need to ensure the proper enforcement of EC law while still respecting the autonomy of the Member States, the ECJ has laid down a number of guidelines that the national courts are obliged to take into account. The first of these is the principle of non-discrimination.

In the *Comet* case, the Court's decision was contingent on 'it being understood that such conditions cannot be less favourable than those relating to similar actions of a domestic nature'.

This means that although the appropriate court and procedures are left up to the Member States, the States still have an obligation to ensure that national procedures do not discriminate against any individual wishing to enforce an EC law, rather than national law, right.

In addition, national procedures must not make it excessively difficult to obtain a remedy for a breach of EC law. In Case 199/82, *Amministrazione delle Finanze dello Stato v San Giorgio* (*San Giorgio*), the ECJ explained that national rules and procedures must not make it, in practice, impossible for rights conferred by the Community to be exercised.

3. Remedies

The ECJ has been particularly careful to ensure that appropriate remedies are available with regard to breaches of Community law rules. In Case 33/76, *Rewe-Zentralfinanz v Landschwirtschaftskammer*, the Court explained that although it has been made possible for individuals to bring direct actions based on EC law before national courts, 'it was not intended to create new remedies in the national courts to ensure the observance of Community law.'

Consequently, the remedies available for similar breaches of national law should be made available for breaches of EC law. However, once more, this has been qualified by guidelines laid down in decisions of the ECJ. The provision of a remedy must not discriminate and must be made available 'on the same conditions as would apply were it a question of observing national law' (*Rewe-Zentralfinanz*). In addition, the remedy made available under national law must be an effective remedy.

In Case 14/83, *Von Colson*, the ECJ explained that Art 10 EC (then Art 5) provides Member States, and therefore their national courts, with the obligation of facilitating the achievement of the aims of the Community. Consequently, Member States and national courts must ensure that remedies available for breaches of EC law must be 'effective', have a 'deterrent effect' and be 'adequate in relation to the damage sustained' (in other words, be proportionate).

The Court developed this principle in Case 222/84, *Johnston v Chief Constable of the RUC*, emphasising the need to ensure effective judicial protection for those who have suffered as a result of a breach of Community law. It was in Case C-271/91, *Marshall v Southampton and South West Hampshire AHA* (*Marshall* (*No 2*)) that the ECJ took the principle of effectiveness a step further by providing that not only did the remedy have to be comparable with that available for a similar breach of national law (*Comet and Rewe-Zentralfinanz*) but, if no effective remedy was available under national law, national courts should either improve upon what was available or devise a new, suitable remedy.

4. The development of a uniform Community remedy

In general, the Community has been happy to allow national courts to protect the Community law rights of individuals by means of appropriate national procedures and remedies. There has, however, been one exception to this: the development of the Community remedy of State damages.

The development of this remedy has been considered in some detail in Chapter 4. To briefly recap, in Cases C-6 and 9/90, *Francovich*, the ECJ provided that where a Member State had failed to correctly implement the aims of a directive, damages were available from the State to compensate those who had suffered loss as a result of the State's breach. This ensures that Member States may not rely on, or benefit from, their own wrongdoings and that the remedy for doing so is uniform throughout the Community.

The remedy is based on the obligations placed on Member States by Art 10 EC and has been developed in later cases (particularly Cases C-46 and 48/93, *Brasserie du Pêcheur* and *Factortame*) to include *any* sufficiently serious breach of Community law by a State or its public bodies. A number

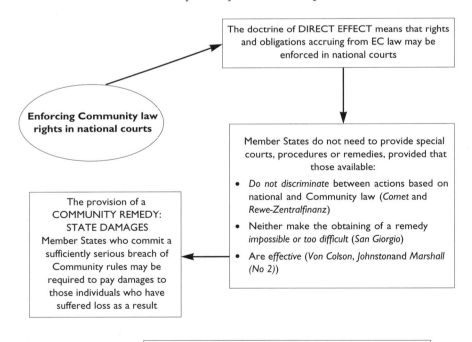

The doctrine of DIRECT EFFECT means that rights and obligations accruing from EC law may be enforced in national courts

Enforcing Community law rights in national courts

Member States do not need to provide special courts, procedures or remedies, provided that those available:

- *Do not discriminate* between actions based on national and Community law (*Comet* and *Rewe-Zentralfinanz*)
- Neither make the obtaining of a remedy *impossible or too difficult* (*San Giorgio*)
- Are *effective* (*Von Colson, Johnston* and *Marshall (No 2)*)

The provision of a COMMUNITY REMEDY: STATE DAMAGES Member States who commit a sufficiently serious breach of Community rules may be required to pay damages to those individuals who have suffered loss as a result

Community Rights and National Courts

of criteria must be fulfilled before damages can be made available and these too are considered in Chapter 4.

II. PRELIMINARY REFERENCES/RULINGS

Article 234 EC provides the ECJ with the jurisdiction to give preliminary rulings on the interpretation of the Treaty and also on the interpretation *and validity* of secondary legislation, when requested to do so by national courts.

1. The purpose of preliminary rulings

The purpose of Art 234 EC is to ensure the uniform interpretation and application of Community law. The principle of direct effect has firmly established national courts as enforcers of EC law and if interpretation were left to the courts of the Member States, it would not be possible to ensure uniformity, given that different legal systems employ different interpretative methods. (Consider, for example, the position in the United Kingdom, where the literal method of interpretation is favoured, as opposed to other Member States, who may employ a more purposive approach.)

2. The effects of preliminary rulings

The ECJ is not bound by precedent. It does not have to follow its own previous rulings but in reality it does so in order to ensure consistency (the Court's dicta in Cases 28–30/62, *Da Costa*, in which the ECJ repeated its *Van Gend* judgement, is a good example of this).

A referring national court will, however, be bound by the ruling of the ECJ and is obliged to apply the ruling obtained to the case before it. While a ruling will normally be retrospective in its effect, the ECJ may limit the temporal effects of any such ruling (as it did in Case C-262/88, *Barber v Guardian Royal Exchange*, where the Court held that the ruling was effective only from the date of its judgement).

Despite national courts being bound by the ECJ, the Court has taken pains to point out that it is not 'senior' to the national courts, but merely has a different function to perform. In reality, however, the ECJ undoubtedly enjoys a superior position, to employing national courts as enforcers or 'appliers' of Community law.

3. Which national bodies may make a reference?

Article 234 EC provides that 'any court or tribunal of a Member State' may make a reference. The ECJ has accepted references from a variety of courts and tribunals, including arbitration panels, insurance officers and administrative tribunals (the reference in *Van Gend* came from a Dutch Administrative Tribunal). Consideration of case law demonstrates, however, that the ECJ does not have the jurisdiction to accept a reference from a body that lies wholly or partially outside the legal systems of the Member States. In Case 102/81, *Nordsee*, for example, a request for a ruling was made by an arbitration tribunal that had been established by contract – the reference was consequently refused. Conversely, in Case 246/80, *Broekmeulen*, the ECJ considered that a Dutch body known as the Appeals Committee for General Medicine was an appropriate body, as it operated with the consent and co-operation of the public authorities and delivered decisions which were recognised as final in law.

4. The decision to refer

A national court or tribunal will only need to make a reference where it considers that its decision in the immediate case rests on a point of Community law. Article 234 EC makes it clear that it is for the national court to decide when a reference is to be made and not the parties to a case or any other party or authority, including the ECJ. (National precedent should never operate to prevent a court from seeking a ruling, as evidenced by Cases 146 and 166/73, *Rheinmuhlen-Dusseldorf*.) The Treaty also distinguishes between those national courts that have the discretion to refer and those that are obliged to.

i. The discretion to refer

Article 234(2) provides that any court 'may, if it considers that a decision on the question is necessary to enable it to give judgement, request the Court of Justice to give a ruling thereon'. The ECJ has interpreted this to mean that where an appropriate body is called upon to reach a decision which is based on an issue of Community law, that body has the right to make a reference to the ECJ (Case 92/78, *Simmenthal*). It should be noted, however, that where the action concerns the validity of secondary legislation, such discretion will be lost unless the Court is satisfied that the Community act is valid. This is because the ECJ alone has the jurisdiction to declare a Community act invalid (Case 314/85, *Foto-Frost*).

ii. The obligation to refer

Article 234(3) EC provides that national courts or tribunals 'against whose decisions there is no judicial remedy in national law ... *shall* bring the matter before the Court of Justice'. Thus, any court from which there is no appeal *must* make a reference when called upon to reach a decision on a matter which relates to a point of Community law. There are, however, conflicting opinions as to which courts this obligation applies.

Under what has become known as the 'abstract theory', only courts from which there is no appeal will be obliged to refer (in the United Kingdom, for example, Lord Denning in *Bulmer v Bollinger* (1974) considered that only the House of Lords fell into this category). Under the 'concrete theory', it is, however, thought that where the parties have no automatic right of appeal, the national court is obliged to refer. This theory is the most persuasive and is supported by the ECJ, as can be evidenced by reference to *Costa v ENEL*.

It should be noted that there are three circumstances in which the ECJ has specifically held that it may not be necessary for a national court to make a reference. These circumstances were explained by the Court in Case 283/81, *CILFIT*,* and are as follows:

- the question of EC law is irrelevant to the case being heard by the national court;
- the question of EC law has already been interpreted by the ECJ in a previous ruling (this principle was first established in *Da Costa*. As the ECJ does not have to follow its own previous rulings, national courts should, however, recognise the possibility that the ECJ may amend its original ruling and bear this in mind when taking their decision as to whether to refer or not);
- the correct interpretation is so obvious as to leave no scope for reasonable doubt (known as *acte clair* in the French legal system).

This has been supported in cases such as Case C-99/00 *Kenny Roland Lyckeskog*, where the parties always had a right of appeal to the (Swedish)

---

* It should be noted that the ECJ has not precluded national courts from making a reference in the above circumstances; it has merely removed the obligation.

Supreme Court. However, the ECJ has since explained that where a national court *is* under an obligation to refer (i.e. none of the above 'exceptions' apply) but does *not*, the State may be liable in damages (under the principle of *Francovich* or State Damages, Chapter 5) for the failure of that court. (Case C-224/01, *Kobler v Austria*.)

5. Can the ECJ refuse to provide a ruling?

As already considered, the decision to refer is the national courts' alone and may not be questioned by the ECJ. The ECJ has, however, on occasion, declined to give a ruling.

We have already considered instances where the Court has refused a ruling due to the fact that the national body making the ruling lay outside the Member State's legal system. In addition, in Cases 104/79 and 244/80, *Foglia v Novello* (*Nos 1 and 2*), the ECJ concluded that it had no jurisdiction to provide a ruling in a dispute which had been 'fabricated' by the parties, as their role was not to give abstract or advisory opinions. In Case C-83/91, *Meilicke*, the Court similarly concluded that it would exceed its jurisdiction if it answered hypothetical questions.

It has also withheld its opinion where proceedings have terminated in the national court (Case 338/85, *Pardini*) and also when it has felt that it has been given insufficient information or the question was too vague (the Court has now issued guidance on this matter in 'Guidance on references by national courts for preliminary rulings' [1997] 1 CMLR 78).

From examination of the above and other case law, it can be concluded that the ECJ may refuse to provide a ruling, but only in circumstances where to provide such a ruling would amount to an abuse of the preliminary reference procedure.

6. The referral procedure

Where a national court reaches the conclusion that a reference is appropriate, it must formulate a question or questions to refer to the ECJ. (Where such questions are in some way inappropriate, the ECJ in the past has shown itself willing to reformulate them in a manner that will best assist the national court, although there is growing evidence that the Court is becoming less willing to do this due, perhaps, to pressure of work.)

The national court will also need to provide issues of fact and national law relevant to the case in question. The national court will stay proceedings until the ruling of the ECJ is transmitted back to it. Being of general interest, once the ECJ has received a reference, it will be translated into all official languages of the Community, notified to the Member States and Community institutions and noted in the Official Journal. Written observations will be accepted from the parties, Member States and institutions, and there will be a brief opportunity for oral submissions to be put before the Court (these will be in the official language of the national court that referred the question). The ECJ will deliberate the matter, after receiving the opinion of the AG, finally providing a judgement which will be reached by majority vote. This decision will then not only be returned to the national court, but also published in the Reports of Cases.

It is important to remember that, while the ECJ has jurisdiction to pronounce on the validity of EC secondary legislation and interpret the Treaty, it is not the function of the Court to decide the outcome of the case before the national court. The national court must perform this function.

i. The consequences of the preliminary reference procedure

The availability of preliminary references has had a number of important consequences.

First, it has forged a link between national legal systems and the EC legal system. Without such rulings, national courts and the ECJ would remain isolated from one another. Second, the availability of a reference affords national courts the opportunity to familiarise themselves with the Community legal order.

Of particular importance is the manner in which the ECJ has used the process in order to develop the EC's legal system and constitutionalise the Treaties. The Court has clarified the extent of Community law through its development of principles such as direct effect and supremacy in seminal judgements such as *Van Gend* and *Costa* (discussed in Chapter 5). In addition, preliminary references have been the vehicle by which the general principles of EC law have been articulated (Chapter 4).

In conjunction with Art 10 EC, the Court has also been able to further extend the scope and effectiveness of the Community's legal order, developing such principles as the 'interpretative obligation' (*Von Colson*) and 'State damages' (*Francovich*). Further protection has been afforded to individuals by the Court, which has ensured, for example, that the remedies available for breach of Community law rights are effective (as in *Marshall* (*No 2*)) and available to as many citizens as possible (such as in *Hoekstra*, discussed in Chapter 8).

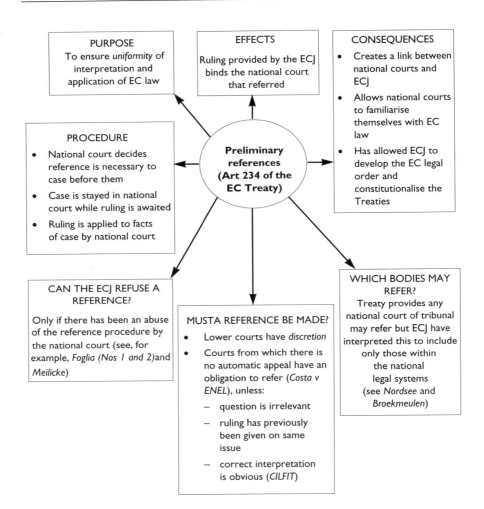

PURPOSE
To ensure *uniformity* of interpretation and application of EC law

EFFECTS
Ruling provided by the ECJ binds the national court that referred

CONSEQUENCES
- Creates a link between national courts and ECJ
- Allows national courts to familiarise themselves with EC law
- Has allowed ECJ to develop the EC legal order and constitutionalise the Treaties

PROCEDURE
- National court decides reference is necessary to case before them
- Case is stayed in national court while ruling is awaited
- Ruling is applied to facts of case by national court

Preliminary references (Art 234 of the EC Treaty)

CAN THE ECJ REFUSE A REFERENCE?
Only if there has been an abuse of the reference procedure by the national court (see, for example, *Foglia (Nos 1 and 2)*and *Meilicke*)

MUSTA REFERENCE BE MADE?
- Lower courts have *discretion*
- Courts from which there is no automatic appeal have an obligation to refer (*Costa v ENEL*), unless:
  - question is irrelevant
  - ruling has previously been given on same issue
  - correct interpretation is obvious (*CILFIT*)

WHICH BODIES MAY REFER?
Treaty provides any national court of tribunal may refer but ECJ have interpreted this to include only those within the national legal systems (see *Nordsee* and *Broekmeulen*)

III. ENFORCEMENT ACTIONS AGAINST MEMBER STATES

Article 10 EC clearly provides all Member States with the duty to fulfil the specific obligations placed on them by both the Treaty and secondary sources of Community law. It also provides the Member States with a general duty not to do anything that could jeopardise the aims of the Community. It is therefore necessary to consider how the Treaty ensures that all Member States comply with their Community obligations.

1. Actions brought by the Commission (Art 226 EC)

Should a Member State breach EC law and an individual suffer as a result, that individual may, of course, bring an action against the errant State under the doctrine of direct effect (Chapter 5). The Treaty, however, provides other methods of ensuring that Member States comply with their obligations.

The Treaty entrusts the Commission, under Art 211 EC, with the task of ensuring 'the proper functioning and development of the common market'. Article 226 EC expands this duty, giving the Commission the authority to investigate and, if necessary, bring before the ECJ any Member State that it considers may have failed to fulfil its Treaty obligations. The Commission's powers are, however, discretionary and the Institution cannot be forced to act against a Member State (Case 48/65, *Lutticke*), although the Commission's conduct may be the subject of a complaint to the European Ombudsman (Art 195 EC).

It is perfectly possible for an individual to bring an action against a Member State while, at the same time, the Commission is also initiating enforcement proceedings. This can be evidenced by the *Factortame* series of cases, together with Case C-246/89R, *Commission v UK*. Both acts and omissions of the Member States are open to scrutiny (Case 167/73, *Commission v France*).

Investigations under Art 226 EC are initiated by the Commission, either on its own initiative or following a complaint (it should be noted that the complainant does not play any further role in the proceedings, as they are not intended as a means by which individuals can obtain redress). Actions may be divided into two stages – the administrative stage and the judicial stage. The administrative stage can be further subdivided into the informal and the formal.

i. The Commission's investigative powers

Where the Commission suspects a Member State is in breach of its Community obligations, the Commission will enter into (informal) dialogue with the appropriate authorities within that State. This stage is very important, as the majority of alleged breaches are resolved without the need for further intervention by the Commission. (It would appear that many states fail to comply with their obligations due to ignorance or misunderstanding and, in such circumstances, they are normally quick to remedy their breach.)

If the alleged breach is not rectified at this stage, the Commission may issue a formal letter, defining the breach and requesting that the Member

State submit its observations within a reasonable amount of time (normally two months). If the issue remains unresolved at the end of this period, the Commission will deliver a 'reasoned opinion', setting out how the Member State has violated its Community law obligations and allowing it a reasonable time (again usually two months, but this will depend on individual circumstances) to remedy the alleged breach. The reasoned opinion is very important in that it establishes the scope of the action and the legal arguments on which the Commission is relying. Should the Commission attempt to change its arguments at a later date, these will be rejected by the ECJ.

ii. Judicial proceedings

If the breach is not remedied within the stated time, the Commission will proceed to the judicial stage, referring the matter to the ECJ. Even at this stage, it may be possible to settle the action before the Court gives its judgement. Where judgement is given, only about one in 10 decisions favour the Member State. This is not surprising, as the Commission is unlikely to proceed if its case is weak. In addition, the ECJ has shown itself unreceptive to the majority of defences argued by the Member State.

In Case 128/78, *Commission v UK* (the *Tachograph* case) for example, the United Kingdom argued 'practical difficulties' due to trade union resistance to the introduction of tachographs in the cabs of lorries, while in Cases 227–30/85, *Commission v Belgium*, it was argued that failure of regional, rather than central government had caused the breach. The Court accepted neither argument. In Case 101/84, *Commission v Italy*, Italy did not submit statistics required by the Community as a bomb attack on a data processing centre had destroyed relevant data. Italy argued *force majeure*, which was again not accepted by the Court (the ECJ did, however, concede that, in certain circumstances, this may provide an acceptable defence).

iii. Non-compliance with the Court's judgement

If the ECJ finds that a Member State is in breach of its Community obligations, it will issue a declaration to that effect, requiring that the breach be *immediately* remedied. Until amendments made by the TEU were introduced, the judgements of the ECJ were of declaratory effect only, the only remedy for failure to comply being the possibility of further enforcement proceedings being initiated by the Commission.

Under the amended Art 228, the Commission may, *after bringing further enforcement proceedings* and on referral to the Court, specify an appropriate pecuniary penalty (fine) to be levied against the errant Member State. This has had the effect of providing an originally rather toothless action with the necessary teeth, although it is not yet clear what the outcome would be if a Member State refused to pay any fine imposed. This question has been the topic of academic debate, with a favoured suggestion being the removal of a defaulting Member State's voting rights within the Council. No State has yet refused to pay, however.

2. Actions brought by Member States

If one Member State considers that another Member State has failed to fulfil its Community obligations, then the first State may bring the matter before the ECJ under Art 227 EC. The procedure first requires that the matter be brought to the attention of the Commission. Proceedings will then mirror those contained under Art 226, other than the requirement that the Commission request the observations of both Member States.

The Commission is required to deliver a reasoned opinion within three months of the matter being brought to its attention. If the Commission fails to provide a reasoned opinion within this time, the complainant Member State may bring the matter before the ECJ. Should the Court find a violation, matters proceed as discussed above.

Actions brought under Art 227 EC are extremely rare, with judgement only being reached on one occasion (Case 141/78, *France v UK*). This is understandable, as Member States prefer to make an informal complaint to the Commission, rather than choose the far more politically contentious Art 227 route.

3. The effectiveness of enforcement procedures

Although no official figures are available relating the success of the informal investigative stage followed by the Commission, the administrative stage as a whole is particularly successful in resolving breaches, as reference to the following table demonstrates:

Year	Formal letters issued	Reasoned opinions issued	Referrals to the ECJ
1999	1,075	460	178
2000	1,317	460	172
2001	1,050	569	162

As the above figures demonstrate, the vast majority of breaches are resolved without the need to refer the matter to the ECJ. This suggests that the administrative stage of enforcement procedures is particularly successful in that it allows the Commission to 'educate' Member States and ensure that they are aware of their EC obligations.

However, also important with regard to the effectiveness of enforcement actions is the Commission's ability – or lack of it – to uncover

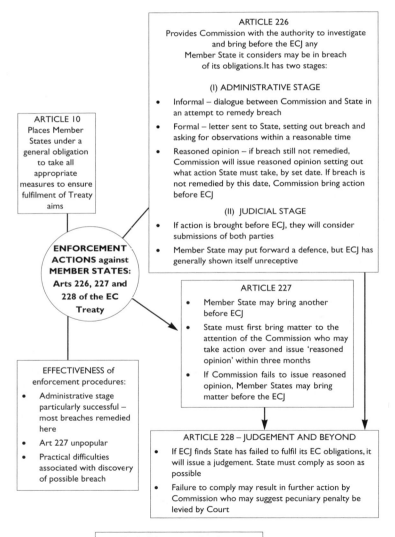

ARTICLE 226
Provides Commission with the authority to investigate and bring before the ECJ any Member State it considers may be in breach of its obligations. It has two stages:

(I) ADMINISTRATIVE STAGE

- Informal – dialogue between Commission and State in an attempt to remedy breach
- Formal – letter sent to State, setting out breach and asking for observations within a reasonable time
- Reasoned opinion – if breach still not remedied, Commission will issue reasoned opinion setting out what action State must take, by set date. If breach is not remedied by this date, Commission bring action before ECJ

(II) JUDICIAL STAGE

- If action is brought before ECJ, they will consider submissions of both parties
- Member State may put forward a defence, but ECJ has generally shown itself unreceptive

ARTICLE 10
Places Member States under a general obligation to take all appropriate measures to ensure fulfilment of Treaty aims

ENFORCEMENT ACTIONS against MEMBER STATES: Arts 226, 227 and 228 of the EC Treaty

ARTICLE 227

- Member State may bring another before ECJ
- State must first bring matter to the attention of the Commission who may take action over and issue 'reasoned opinion' within three months
- If Commission fails to issue reasoned opinion, Member States may bring matter before the ECJ

EFFECTIVENESS of enforcement procedures:

- Administrative stage particularly successful – most breaches remedied here
- Art 227 unpopular
- Practical difficulties associated with discovery of possible breach

ARTICLE 228 – JUDGEMENT AND BEYOND

- If ECJ finds State has failed to fulfil its EC obligations, it will issue a judgement. State must comply as soon as possible
- Failure to comply may result in further action by Commission who may suggest pecuniary penalty be levied by Court

Enforcement Actions

possible breaches. The Commission has no 'police force' that it can enlist to assist in the uncovering of breaches by the Member States and it is likely that very many continue unnoticed. In recognition of this, the Commission has employed technology to encourage citizens and companies to notify them of possible breaches on their website.

The Commission has also recognised that, often, a State's breach will be the result of their failure to implement directives. The Commission has sought to remedy this by requiring that directives be published in the Official Journal and also by insisting that Member States notify them when directives are incorporated into national law.

It can be concluded that enforcement procedures, particularly the administrative stage of Art 226 EC, play an important role in ensuring that Community aims are achieved and Community law is upheld.

IV. ACTIONS AGAINST THE COMMUNITY INSTITUTIONS: JUDICIAL REVIEW

The Treaty provides the Community institutions with a number of powers and obligations. As in all developed legal systems, a mechanism has been put into place through which the manner in which these obligations are discharged can be reviewed.

'Judicial review' is the term commonly used to describe a variety of causes of action relating to the review of acts or decisions of the Community institutions. It includes annulment actions (Art 230 EC) and actions for failure to act (Art 232 EC). 'Judicial review' also covers applications for interim measures relating to other judicial procedures (Art 243 EC). These procedures are part of the system of 'checks and balances' which exist to ensure that Community institutions act within the limits of the powers afforded them by the Treaties.

1. Actions to annul Community Acts (Art 230 EC)

Article 230 is the primary Community method by which the legality of the acts of the Community institutions may be challenged. If such a challenge is successful, the act will be declared void by the ECJ (Art 231 EC).

i. Whose acts may be challenged?

Article 230 EC refers to 'acts adopted jointly by the European Parliament and the Council, acts of the Council, of the Commission and of the ECB... and of the European Parliament intended to produce legal effects vis à vis third parties'. Prior to amendments introduced by the TEU, the Treaty only referred to acts adopted by the Council and the Commission. The ECJ had, however, already declared the acts of the European Parliament (EP) to be reviewable prior to such amendments (see Case 294/83, *Parti Ecologiste 'Les Verts' v European Parliament* – both this decision and the subsequent Treaty amendments can be seen as an example of the increasing recognition of the importance of the role played by the EP within the Community).

ii. Which acts may be challenged?

Consideration of the wording of Art 230 EC reveals that acts (regulations, decisions and directives) other than recommendations and opinions may be challenged. The ECJ has interpreted this broadly to include any act which is capable of having legal effects (see, for example, Case 22/70, *Commission v Council*, the *ERTA* case).

iii. Grounds for bringing a challenge

The Treaty specifies the following grounds under which an action may be brought:

- lack of competence – this occurs where the Community institutions act in areas where they are not authorised to do so by the Treaty;
- infringement of an essential procedural requirement – for example, the Council failing to consult the EP, as in Case 138/79, *Roquette Frères v Council*;
- infringement of the Treaty or any rule of law relating to its application – this ground often overlaps with others. The ECJ has explained that it can include a breach of one of the general principles of Community law – see Case 4/73, *Nold v Commission*;
- misuse of powers – this ground will be relevant where an institution has used its power(s) for an improper purpose.

iv. Who can bring such an action?

This has proved to be a controversial area and often the subject of examination questions. Applicants can be divided into those with automatic *locus standi* (see Glossary) and those who have to prove sufficient interest and can be categorised as follows.

Privileged applicants

The Treaty gives automatic *locus standi* to Member States, the Council of the EU, the Commission and, since amendments introduced by the ToN, the EP (this is once more an example of the increasing power of the EP. As already discussed above, the position of the EP as a litigant was amended by the TEU. While the ECJ had already accepted the Parliament's right to bring an action in Case C-70/88, *European Parliament v Council* (the *Chernobyl* case), it was not until the TEU came into force that this was formalised).

Semi-privileged applicants

In cases where their prerogatives (rights or interests) are clearly affected, the Treaty provides that the CoA and ECB may commence an action.

Non-privileged applicants

The Treaty provides that any natural or legal person (that is, an individual or company) may bring an action where he is the *addressee* of a decision and there is little problem demonstrating *locus standi* in such a situation.

However, the Treaty also provides that where a decision has been addressed to another person or the act in question is a regulation, which in the circumstances is equivalent to a decision, that person may bring an action providing that it can be demonstrated that the act affects him both directly and individually. (Note that natural and legal persons may not challenge directives.)

It therefore needs to be considered how 'direct and individual concern' has been interpreted by the ECJ in relation to both decisions and regulations.

Individual concern – Where the act in question is a decision addressed to another, the ECJ has developed a 'test' to ascertain individual concern, often referred to as the '*Plaumann* Formula'. In Case 25/62, *Plaumann v Commission* the applicant was a clementine importer. He sought to challenge a decision addressed to the German Government, as it allowed Germany to amend the duty on clementines imported from outside the EC. The ECJ prescribed that, in order to demonstrate 'individual concern', the applicant must be able to show that he was distinguishable from other persons generally, due to certain attributes or circumstances: in other words, he had to show he was a member of a 'closed class'. In addition, he was required to demonstrate that, by virtue of those attributes or circumstances, he should be singled out in the same way as the addressee of the directive.

Plaumann failed in his action because, as the Court pointed out, any other person could, if they wished, carry out the commercial activity in which he was involved and he was consequently not held to be part of a 'closed class'. The test has been confirmed in a number of cases and, for example, those who have entered into a contract (Case 11/82, *Piraiki-Patraiki v Commission*) and those who have applied for a licence (Cases 106 & 107/63, *Toepfer v Commisson*) have been held to come within the necessary 'closed class'.

This test has, however, been criticised as unduly restrictive but *Plaumann* remains the seminal case in this area, despite being the recent subject of much judicial activity and academic speculation. In March 2002, AG Jacobs delivered an Opinion in Case C-50/00P, *Union de Pequeños Agricultores v Council* (the *UPA* case), in which he proposed that there be a redefinition of the test for 'individual concern'. A short time later, the CFI appeared to support this approach in Case T-177/01, *Jégo Quéré v Commission*, also suggesting that the rather narrow definition provided in Plaumann be broadened and made easier to satisfy. The ECJ, however, rejected the positions of both the AG and the CFI, arguing that it was not for them to reform the conditions for *locus standi* but that it should be a matter for legislation.

It has been argued that this is rather a surprising stance for the ECJ to take, given its previous willingness in other areas, to ensure citizens have sufficient opportunity to enforce their rights. It has also been pointed out that there is nothing in the wording of Art 230 to suggest that such a restrictive interpretation be provided. Where the legislative act in question is a regulation, the Court has explained that it will look behind the form of the act to the substance in order to determine its true nature (e.g. Cases 41–44/70, *International Fruit Co v Commission*).

This ensures that the institutions cannot reduce the opportunity for challenge by choosing a legislative form that is not open to question by individuals. The same 'closed category' test as in *Plaumann* will be applied to demonstrate 'individual concern'. (Case C-309/89, *Cordoniu v Council*, and in Cases 789 and 790/79, *Calpak*).

'Direct' concern – Where an applicant succeeds in demonstrating 'individual concern', he must also prove that the act was of 'direct concern' to him. According to the ECJ's interpretation, this requires that the applicant show that (1) the act has directly affected his legal position

and (2) a direct link exists between the act complained of and the loss/damage suffered, which can be compared to demonstrating 'causation' under English and Welsh law. (An illustrative case is *International Fruit Co v Commission*).

The ECJ has provided that the measure can only be of direct concern where no discretion is afforded to the Member State(s) with regard to its implementation (in Cases 10 and 18/68, *Eridania v Commission*, for example, a Commission Decision relating to the provision of aid was considered not to be of direct concern as authority relating to the allocation of such aid was given to the State).

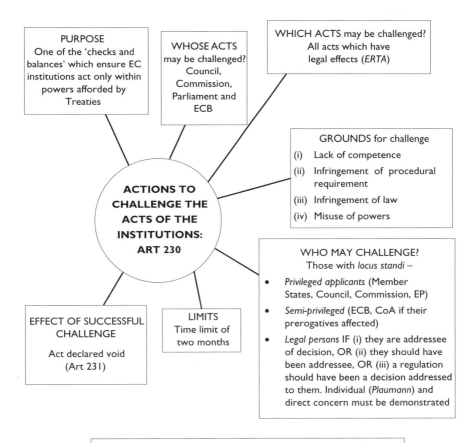

PURPOSE
One of the 'checks and balances' which ensure EC institutions act only within powers afforded by Treaties

WHOSE ACTS
may be challenged?
Council,
Commission,
Parliament and
ECB

WHICH ACTS may be challenged?
All acts which have legal effects (*ERTA*)

ACTIONS TO CHALLENGE THE ACTS OF THE INSTITUTIONS: ART 230

GROUNDS for challenge
(i)   Lack of competence
(ii) Infringement of procedural requirement
(iii) Infringement of law
(iv) Misuse of powers

WHO MAY CHALLENGE?
Those with *locus standi* –
• *Privileged applicants* (Member States, Council, Commission, EP)
• *Semi-privileged* (ECB, CoA if their prerogatives affected)
• *Legal persons* IF (i) they are addressee of decision, OR (ii) they should have been addressee, OR (iii) a regulation should have been a decision addressed to them. Individual (*Plaumann*) and direct concern must be demonstrated

EFFECT OF SUCCESSFUL CHALLENGE
Act declared void (Art 231)

LIMITS
Time limit of two months

Judicial Review of the Acts of EC Institutions

Time limit

The Treaty imposes a time limit of two months on the bringing of an action. This time starts to run either from the publication of the measure, from its notification to the claimant, or from the day on which it came, or should have come, to the attention of the claimant.

Effects of annulment

Article 231 EC provides that if the Court finds an application for annulment well founded, the act should be declared void. Normally, nullity will be considered to be retroactive, although the Court has shown itself willing to limit the temporal effects in appropriate circumstances, particularly where an innocent party may otherwise suffer loss (e.g. Case 81/72, *Commission v Council*).

Under Art 233 EC, institutions are obliged to act to comply with the judgement of the ECJ. The Treaty does not provide any sanction should an institution fail to comply with a judgement (unlike the position where a Member State fails to comply), although by failing to comply, an institution may find itself vulnerable to claims for damages under Art 288 EC, which is discussed in further detail below.

v. Actions against institutions for failure to act (Art 232 EC)

Actions under Art 232 can be seen as the other side of the coin from actions under Art 230 EC. While the latter renders acts of the institutions ineffective, the former may be used to compel an institution to fulfil its Community obligations. An action will consequently only be available where the applicant can show that such an obligation exists.

Whose failure to act can be challenged?

Article 232 EC clearly provides that 'Should the European Parliament, the Council or the Commission, in infringement of this Treaty, fail to act', an action may be brought before the ECJ. Action may also be brought against the ECB, as prescribed by Art 232(4) EC.

Who may make a challenge?

The Treaty provides the Member States and all institutions with automatic *locus standi*. The ECB may also bring an action if it can be shown that it relates to an area falling within the Bank's 'field of competence'. Natural and legal persons once more have limited *locus standi* and may only bring an action where an institution had an obligation to address an act (other than an opinion or a recommendation) to him, her or it. The applicant must demonstrate direct and individual concern and the Court will apply the same restrictive tests as have been established for Art 230 EC (Case C-107/91, *ENU v Commission*).

vi. Procedure in Art 232

Actions will only be admissible where the institution has first been called upon to act by the challenger, thus providing the institution concerned with the opportunity to remedy its alleged omission.

Once a request for action has been made, the institution must then define its position within two months of being called upon to act. Once an institution has defined its position, no further action is possible – even where the institution fails to act (Case 48/65, *Alfons Lutticke v Commission*) – although the ECJ has, on occasion, been willing to accept a challenge to the definition itself, under Art 230 EC (Case 191/82, *Seed Crushers and Oil Producers Association v Commission*).

If the institution does *not* define its position, any action is then subject to a time limit of a further two months.

2. Consequences of a successful action

Article 233 EC provides that institutions are obliged to comply with the Court's ruling under Art 232 EC.

3. Other actions available against the institutions

It is obvious that bringing an action under either Art 230 or 232 EC can present particular problems for individuals, both natural and legal, due to the difficulties associated with proving *locus standi*. In addition, neither Article provides the opportunity for claiming damages. It is therefore important to consider possible alternatives.

Such actions are considered, albeit briefly, below.

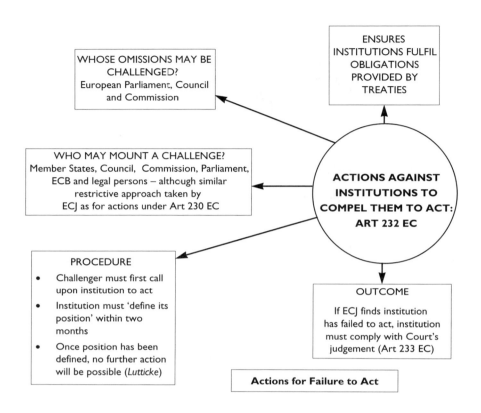

WHOSE OMISSIONS MAY BE CHALLENGED?
European Parliament, Council and Commission

ENSURES INSTITUTIONS FULFIL OBLIGATIONS PROVIDED BY TREATIES

WHO MAY MOUNT A CHALLENGE?
Member States, Council, Commission, Parliament, ECB and legal persons – although similar restrictive approach taken by ECJ as for actions under Art 230 EC

ACTIONS AGAINST INSTITUTIONS TO COMPEL THEM TO ACT: ART 232 EC

PROCEDURE
- Challenger must first call upon institution to act
- Institution must 'define its position' within two months
- Once position has been defined, no further action will be possible (*Lutticke*)

OUTCOME
If ECJ finds institution has failed to act, institution must comply with Court's judgement (Art 233 EC)

Actions for Failure to Act

i. Preliminary references

As has already been considered above, the preliminary reference procedure (Art 234 EC) allows national courts to question the validity of Community acts. While preliminary references do *not* provide individuals with a direct action, they may nevertheless provide a channel through which an indirect challenge may be mounted and, as such, should be borne in mind.

4. Plea of illegality (Art 241 EC)

Article 241 EC provides a means of indirect challenge against a Community regulation but, once more, the Court will look at the substance rather than the form of the act (Case 92/78, *Simmenthal*).

A plea of illegality is not an independent action (Cases 31 and 33/62, *Wohrmann and Lutticke v Commission*). It is only available as a defence, where other proceedings have been brought against the applicant, and the ECJ has explained that the purpose of the action is to allow individuals' protection from the application of an illegal regulation. The action may be pleaded on the same grounds as those found under Art 230 EC.

The effect of a successful challenge is that the regulation will be declared inapplicable in that case, but it will not be declared void. Any measures based on the regulation will, however, be automatically void and subsequent measures based on the regulation will also be open to challenge.

5. Actions for damages (Art 288 EC)

i. Contractual liability

Article 288(1) EC provides that the 'contractual liability of the Community shall be governed by the law applicable to the contract in question.' When an individual wishes to make a claim against a Community institution for damages in relation to a contractual matter, the action must therefore be brought in the appropriate national court and under the legal rules appropriate to that Member State.

ii. Non-contractual liability

Article 288(2) EC relates to the Community's non-contractual liability. Under the jurisdiction afforded to it by Art 235 EC, the ECJ may hear

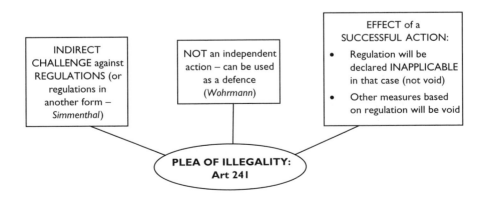

actions brought against the Community in relation to damage caused by its institutions and the ECB (*fautes de service*) or by its servants (*fautes personnelles*) in the performance of their duties.

Actions brought under Art 288 are independent actions and there is no limitation on who may bring such an action (*Lutticke*). However, a time limit of five years from time of injury, or from the time which the claimant should have reasonably known of it, has been imposed. Fault, damage and causation must be proven and as such, an Art 288 action is essentially similar to the English concept of tort.

With regard to liability in relation to 'servants in the performance of their duties', the Community and its institutions may be deemed liable under the concept of vicarious liability. The concept of vicarious liability has been interpreted far more restrictively under Community law than is usual under English law and the range of acts performed by staff for which the Community will accept liability is narrow (as can be evidenced by Case 9/69, *Sayag v Leduc*).

Injurious acts may either be of an administrative or legislative nature and each needs to be considered in turn with regard to the proving of 'fault'.

iii. Administrative acts

Where an action is brought in relation to the manner in which Community rules have been applied or the manner in which staff have carried out their duties, the Community, via the appropriate institution(s) and staff, may be liable for both wrongful acts and omissions.

'Fault' (or 'illegality' as it is sometimes termed) may involve negligence, the failure to consider relevant facts, to accord individuals certain procedural rights or to adequately supervise bodies to whom power has been delegated and so on, and the relative seriousness of the 'error' may be taken into account (e.g. Case 145/83, *Adams v Commission*).

iv. Legislative acts

Where the act complained of is legislative in nature (once again, the substance of the act rather than the form will be decisive), the Court has developed a 'formula', laying down the general conditions which must exist before liability will be found. This formula has become known as the '*Schoppenstedt* formula', following Case 5/71, *Schoppenstedt v Commission*, and involves the following considerations:

- does the legislative act involve choices (that is, discretion) of economic policy on the part of the Community authorities? If yes;

- has there been a breach of a superior rule of law intended for the protection of individuals? If yes;
- is the breach 'sufficiently serious'?

A 'superior rule of law' may be a general principle of Community law, such as non-discrimination or legal certainty. Whether the breach was 'sufficiently serious' (or 'manifest and grave') will depend on a number of factors being taken into consideration. These are likely to include the clarity of the rule that was breached, the amount of discretion enjoyed by the authorities, whether the error was excusable and whether the breach was voluntary or intentional.

In addition to proving fault, a claimant must also demonstrate causation and damage. With regard to causation, the Court has made it clear that the applicant must demonstrate two things:

- the Community action caused the loss/damage;
- the chain of causation has not been broken.

With regard to the second element, the chain of causation may be broken by the actions of a Member State, in which case, it will be the State, as opposed to the Community, that will be liable, unless the Community has failed to adequately exercise its supervisory power over the State (*Lutticke*). If there is joint liability on the part of the Community and a Member State, the Member State will generally be considered to be primarily liable and

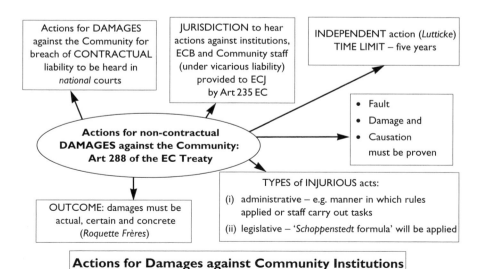

Actions for Damages against Community Institutions

the action should then be brought in the appropriate national court. Contributory negligence may also serve to defeat a claim or at least reduce the quantum of damages (*Adams*).

Article 288 EC provides that the Community must make good 'any damage' caused by its institutions or staff. This has been read restrictively by the Court, which has held that the amount claimed must be actual, certain and concrete (Case 26/74, *Société Roquette Frères v Commission*) and compensation is therefore unlikely to be awarded for losses such as anticipated profits.

It will be evident from the above discussion that liability for damage caused to individuals by a legislative act of one or more of the Community institutions bears a strong resemblance to the application of principle of 'State liability/damages' available against the Member States (discussed in Chapter 5).

Finally, it should be noted that an action for damages may be brought independently or in addition to any claim under Arts 230 and 232 EC.

V. CONCLUSIONS

Community law places rights and obligations on individuals, Member States and Community institutions alike. European law would, however, have little effect if such rights and obligations were unenforceable, and so the Community legal system includes a variety of means by which it can be ensured that all comply with EC law.

When an individual (natural or artificial) breaches Community law, he can expect to have an action brought against him in an appropriate national court under the doctrine of direct effect, with domestic courts being 'assisted' by the ECJ under the preliminary reference procedure. (It should be remembered that the ECJ's role does not allow it to 'take over' the proceedings and its role is restricted to providing an interpretation of Community law and/or judgement as to the validity of legislative acts of the institutions.)

When a Member State breaches its obligations, the Treaty provides that the Commission or a second Member State may bring an action before the ECJ in order to ensure compliance. In addition, a Member State may find itself a defendant in an action before a national court under the doctrine of vertical direct effect and/or, where the claimant wishes to pursue an action for damages, under the principle of 'State damages' (*Francovich*). Often, Member States will find themselves the subject of an action brought by an individual in a national court, while at the same time being the subject of an enforcement action by the Commission.

Other than in actions relating to contractual liability, Community institutions will be brought before the European Courts should they breach Community rules. Any challenge to the validity of legally effective acts of the institutions will normally be brought under Art 230 EC (judicial review), although due to the difficulties associated with proving *locus standi*, individuals should also consider the possibility of employing the preliminary reference, plea of illegality and/or 'action for damages' procedures to mount a challenge. Special notice should, however, be taken of the differing effects of these actions.

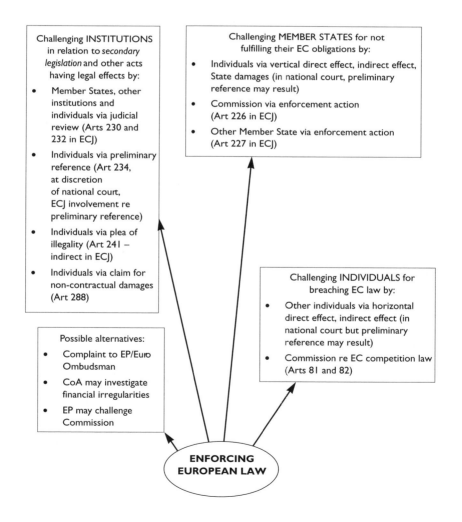

Challenging INSTITUTIONS in relation to *secondary legislation* and other acts having legal effects by:

- Member States, other institutions and individuals via judicial review (Arts 230 and 232 in ECJ)
- Individuals via preliminary reference (Art 234, at discretion of national court, ECJ involvement re preliminary reference)
- Individuals via plea of illegality (Art 241 – indirect in ECJ)
- Individuals via claim for non-contractual damages (Art 288)

Challenging MEMBER STATES for not fulfilling their EC obligations by:

- Individuals via vertical direct effect, indirect effect, State damages (in national court, preliminary reference may result)
- Commission via enforcement action (Art 226 in ECJ)
- Other Member State via enforcement action (Art 227 in ECJ)

Challenging INDIVIDUALS for breaching EC law by:

- Other individuals via horizontal direct effect, indirect effect (in national court but preliminary reference may result)
- Commission re EC competition law (Arts 81 and 82)

Possible alternatives:

- Complaint to EP/Euro Ombudsman
- CoA may investigate financial irregularities
- EP may challenge Commission

ENFORCING EUROPEAN LAW

7 Free Movement of Goods

As previously discussed, the European Communities were created in an attempt to ensure peace and economic stability within Europe and the EC Treaty sets out a number of aims to be achieved, through which these aspirations are to be fulfilled.

While the majority of these aims may be categorised as economic, others have social impacts, while others still can be said to be political in nature. Economic integration is, however, traditionally seen as the primary goal of the Community and the objective of creating a common market has been explicitly set out under Art 2 EC. Article 3 EC enlarges upon this by providing a list of activities that the Community must put into effect in order to ensure that these aims are achieved. Article 3(c) in particular provides that the Community must ensure that all 'obstacles to the free movement of goods, persons, services and capital' are abolished and this is supported by Art 14 EC, which sets out that the Internal Market shall comprise an area without frontiers in which free movement is ensured. These have commonly become known as the 'four freedoms' and it is the first of these freedoms with which this chapter is primarily concerned.

Creating an area that has 'free movement of goods' cannot be achieved overnight and the rules concerning its creation and maintenance are often complex. Such rules can be best understood if an incremental approach is taken and in this chapter, we will consider some of the more important rules which apply to Member States with regard to the removal of both pecuniary and non-pecuniary barriers to trade. Before proceeding we do, however, need to consider how the term 'goods' has been interpreted. Unsurprisingly, a very wide definition has been provided by the ECJ and, in practice, all products which cross an EU border for the purpose of a *commercial* transaction have been declared to be subject to the rules on free movement.

I. THE ELIMINATION OF PECUNIARY (MONETARY) BARRIERS TO TRADE

It should be remembered that prior to the Community's inception, each Member State levied customs duties on goods entering and leaving each State. In order to create an area where trade was facilitated rather than hampered, customs duties had to be removed and a new system of regulation put into place.

1. The creation of a Customs Union and Common Customs Tariff (Arts 23 and 24 EC)

i. What the Treaty says

Article 23 EC provides that the Community is based on a customs union. The creation of a customs union involved the removal of all customs duties, and all charges having equivalent effect, on goods moving between the Member States.

Article 23 EC also provides for the creation of a common customs tariff (CCT). The CCT is charged on all goods imported from outside the Community. It is charged at the same rate no matter which of the Member States the goods are imported into or where they are exported from.

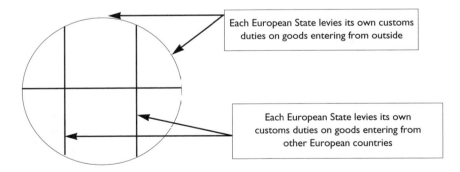

Each European State levies its own customs duties on goods entering from outside

Each European State levies its own customs duties on goods entering from other European countries

Europe PRIOR to the creation of the European Community

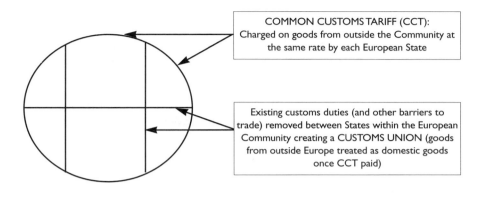

COMMON CUSTOMS TARIFF (CCT):
Charged on goods from outside the Community at
the same rate by each European State

Existing customs duties (and other barriers to
trade) removed between States within the European
Community creating a CUSTOMS UNION (goods
from outside Europe treated as domestic goods
once CCT paid)

**The Common Customs Tariff and the Customs Union
which now exist around and between the Member States**

Article 24 EC also provides that once non-domestically produced goods have been subject to the CCT, they shall be considered to be in free circulation and should be treated no differently than domestic goods. The CCT is a tariff raised by the EC, not Member States and as such forms part of the Community budget. It should not, consequently, be confused with charges levied by the Member States as part of their own internal taxation systems (which are discussed in further detail below). The removal of existing customs duties was not, of course, achieved overnight and it was not until July 1968 that the final remaining customs duties were removed and the CCT was introduced.

2. The prohibition on new customs duties and charges having equivalent effect (Art 25 EC)

The removal of existing customs duties has the obvious benefit of allowing trade to take place on a level playing field, allowing the consumer to be the final arbiter as to which goods will be successful and which less so. The imposition of customs duties may, however, benefit Member States, allowing them an opportunity, for example, to promote domestically manufactured goods over foreign goods via the imposition of high import taxes. Therefore, the possibility of a Member State imposing a new duty or charge could not be ignored.

i. What the Treaty says

The removal of existing pecuniary barriers to trade would not, alone, have ensured the free movement of goods as it would not prevent Member States from re-erecting customs duties or putting into effect other charges having equivalent effect (CHEEs), in circumstances considered beneficial to that State. Article 25 EC consequently provides that: 'Member States shall refrain from introducing between themselves any new customs duties on exports or any charges having equivalent effect.'

ii. The ECJ's interpretation and application of Art 25 EC

Article 25 EC – which applies to both imports and exports alike – appears to provide reasonably clear instruction to Member States, but it has still been necessary for the ECJ to interpret its exact meaning in order to ensure uniform application of its terms.

The term 'goods' is not defined by the Treaty and it has been necessary for the ECJ to consider exactly which goods may be subject to the EC's rules. It is obvious that the free movement of goods is fundamental to the achievement of Community aims and the ECJ has consequently provided a wide interpretation of the term. In Case 7/68, *Commission v Italy* (the *1st Art Treasures* case), the Court defined 'goods' as including products which can be valued in money and which are capable of forming the subject of a commercial transaction.

The Court has also made it clear that the purpose for which the duty or charge is levied is irrelevant and that it is the effect which is significant in deciding whether or not Art 25 EC applies (Case 24/68, *Commission v Italy*, the *2nd Art Treasures* case).

It has also been necessary for the Court to consider which charges will come within the scope of CHEEs. In the *2nd Art Treasures* case, the ECJ once again provided a wide definition, holding CHEEs to include 'any pecuniary charge...imposed...on domestic or foreign goods by reason of the fact that they cross a frontier'.

iii. The 'exceptions' to the rule

Once a duty or charge has been held to come within the scope of Art 25 EC, it is immediately deemed to be unlawful; the Treaty provides no derogation from its prohibitions. The ECJ has, however, explained that certain charges will not come within the scope of Art 25 EC. These include charges levied for a mandatory inspection and charges made for the provision of a commercial service. By providing that such charges may be levied, the ECJ has allowed the Member States to recoup costs which would otherwise have to be borne by the State – rather unfair if the State fails to enjoy a benefit.

Before such a charge will be considered to be outside the scope of Art 25 EC, a number of criteria must be fulfilled:

Charges made for an inspection

Where a Member State levies a charge for an inspection, it will not constitute a CHEE provided it can satisfy the following conditions (Case 18/87, *Commission v Germany*, the *Animal Inspection Fees* case):

- the inspection is mandatory under Community (or international) law (Case 46/76, Bauhuis);
- the inspection is non-discriminatory (that is, both domestic and imported goods treated alike) (Case 87/75, *Bresciani*);
- the inspection is in the interest of the Community and promotes the free movement of goods;
- the charge does not exceed the cost of the inspection (*Bresciani*);
- the charge is proportionate to the quantity of the goods inspected and not their value or quality (*Bresciani*).

Charges levied for a service provided

Where a Member State has levied a charge for a service performed, that charge will not be considered to be a CHEE if the following criteria can be fulfilled (Case 24/68, *Commission v Italy*, the *Statistical Levy* case):

- the service rendered a specific benefit to the importer/exporter (*Statistical Levy* case);
- the charge is proportionate to quantity, not value or quality, of the goods to which the service has been rendered (*Bresciani*);
- the charge does not exceed the cost of the inspection (*Bresciani*);
- both domestic and imported goods are treated alike (*Bresciani*).

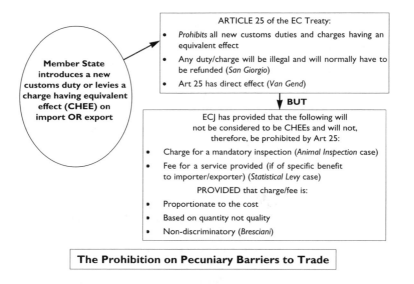

ARTICLE 25 of the EC Treaty:

- *Prohibits* all new customs duties and charges having an equivalent effect
- Any duty/charge will be illegal and will normally have to be refunded (*San Giorgio*)
- Art 25 has direct effect (*Van Gend*)

Member State introduces a new customs duty or levies a charge having equivalent effect (CHEE) on import OR export

BUT

ECJ has provided that the following will not be considered to be CHEEs and will not, therefore, be prohibited by Art 25:

- Charge for a mandatory inspection (*Animal Inspection* case)
- Fee for a service provided (if of specific benefit to importer/exporter) (*Statistical Levy* case)

PROVIDED that charge/fee is:

- Proportionate to the cost
- Based on quantity not quality
- Non-discriminatory (*Bresciani*)

The Prohibition on Pecuniary Barriers to Trade

3. The prohibition on discriminatory internal taxation (Arts 90–93 EC)

As touched on above, the Treaty does not, as yet at least, seek to deprive Member States of the power to levy internal taxes for the purpose of raising public revenue. A genuine tax has been defined as one relating to 'a general system of internal dues applied systematically to categories of products in accordance with objective criteria irrespective of the origin of the products'. However, internal taxation will be unlawful if it discriminates against imported products or is protective of domestic products.

i. What the Treaty says

Article 90 EC provides that: 'No Member State shall impose, directly or indirectly, on the products of other Member States any internal taxation of any kind in excess of that imposed directly or indirectly on similar domestic products.'

Article 90 EC can consequently be seen as complementing the provisions contained in Art 25 EC.

ii. The ECJ's interpretation of Art 90 EC

Clearly, there may be an argument as to what products may be considered to be 'similar'. In Case 27/67, *Fink-Frucht*, the ECJ provided that goods

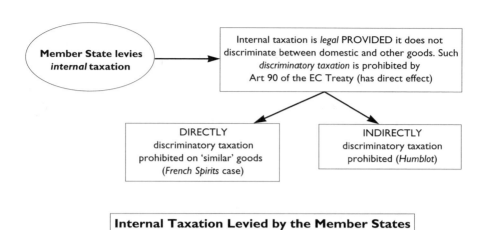

Internal Taxation Levied by the Member States

would be regarded as such if they came within the same tax classification, but it has also been held that products need not necessarily be the same.

For example, in Case 170/78, *Commission v UK*, it was held that beer and wine were sufficiently similar to compete and it can be concluded that an appropriate test may be whether a consumer might substitute one product for the other for the purpose he has in mind. In Case 168/78, *Commission v France*, the *French Spirits* case, characteristics such as composition, physical characteristics and consumer usage were considered.

iii. Indirectly discriminatory internal taxation

Taxation that is directly discriminatory overtly treats domestic and other goods differently, but taxation that is indirectly discriminatory may, on the face of it, appear to comply with Community rules although, in reality, placing non-domestic goods at a disadvantage.

Case 112/84, *Humblot*, provides a good example of such treatment. French law decreed that the amount of car tax payable increased with the power rating of the vehicle, with cars below and above a 16CV rating being charged at different rates. No French car was rated above 16CV and therefore only imported cars fell into the higher tax rating. France's internal car taxation system was therefore considered to be covertly discriminatory.

iv. Enforcing the rules relating to pecuniary barriers to trade

Article 25 EC has been held to be directly effective (*Van Gend*). Traders may therefore enforce their rights against a Member State in the appropriate national court.

Member States will normally be required to repay any charges which have been unlawfully levied (Case 199/82, *Amministrazione delle Finanze dello Stato v San Giorgio*), unless the trader has passed the costs on to his customers (Cases C-192–218/95, *Société Comateb*).

In addition, an errant Member State may find itself the subject of an enforcement action brought by either the Commission or another Member State, before the ECJ (Arts 226–28 EC, discussed in Chapter 6).

Article 90 EC is similarly directly effective (*Humblot*) and individuals may consequently enforce any rights accruing from the Article in their national courts. Once more, Member States who levy discriminatory internal taxation may also find themselves investigated by the Commission.

II. THE ELIMINATION OF NON-PECUNIARY BARRIERS TO TRADE

1. The problem

The prohibition of pecuniary barriers to trade would not, alone, be sufficient to guarantee the free movement of goods within the EC. In addition to the pecuniary measures discussed above, measures of a non-pecuniary nature can also hinder free movement.

Non-pecuniary measures may include quantitative restrictions such as quotas, while the imposition of compulsory inspections or trading rules relating to the composition, packaging and so on of goods may also discourage trade. The Treaty consequently provides a prohibition on quantitative restrictions and measures having equivalent effect.

2. The prohibition of quantitative restrictions and measures having equivalent effect (Arts 28–29 and 30 EC)

Article 28 EC provides that: 'Quantitative restrictions on imports and all measures having equivalent effect shall be prohibited between Member States.' Article 29 EC provides a similar prohibition with regard to exports.

Article 30 EC, on the other hand, provides derogation from both Arts 28 and 29. Such derogation – which may only be claimed in strictly limited circumstances – recognises that some issues are more important than the need to ensure the creation and maintenance of a common market, allowing State regulation and the aim of free movement to be reconciled.

As one would expect, each Member State has developed its own trading rules and, while the Community has attempted to harmonise such rules, progress has been slow. In the absence of harmonising legislation, the ECJ has taken the stance that national rules must not be allowed to hinder the free movement of goods, interpreting Arts 28 and 29 EC broadly to encompass as many restrictive measures as possible. On the other hand, Art 30 EC, which allows Member States to derogate, has been interpreted narrowly, ensuring that as few barriers to trade as possible exist.

3. Article 28 EC

i. Quantitative restrictions

Quantitative restrictions can be described as national measures which impose a numerical limit on goods of a particular type either entering (or leaving) a domestic market. The purpose of such behaviour is often to offer protection to domestic products. Both quotas and total bans fall within the scope of the term (Case 2/73, *Geddo v Ente*, and Case 34/79, *R v Henn and Darby*).

ii. Measures having equivalent effect

As well as prohibiting quantitative restrictions, Art 28 EC outlaws measures having equivalent effect (MHEEs). This term has proved difficult to define and has been the subject of both secondary legislation and numerous interpretations by the ECJ. MHEEs can be seen, however, as including measures which may make importation more difficult or costly, or measures that promote or favour domestic goods.

4. The Commission's view (secondary legislation)

Commission Directive 70/50/EEC (OJ 1097 L13/29) was adopted in an attempt to amplify the meaning of Art 28 EC (then Art 30) and it is still used as a guide to the practices which are subject to Art 28.

The directive makes an important distinction between two types of measures:

- distinctly applicable measures (DAMs) – measures which apply only to imports and are therefore discriminatory; and
- indistinctly applicable measures (IDAMs) – measures which are applicable to both domestic and imported products alike and which therefore are non-discriminatory.

The Commission, by means of the directive, concluded that while discriminatory measures (DAMs) would come within the scope of Art 28 and would consequently be prohibited, non-discriminatory measures (IDAMs) would not normally do so. It is important to note, however, that this has not always been the approach of the ECJ (see below).

5. The jurisprudence of the ECJ

i. Whose 'measures' will be caught?

The Court has provided a wide interpretation with regard to whose measures may be caught by Art 28 EC, which is primarily addressed to Member States.

In Case 113/80, *Commission v Ireland*, the *Buy Irish* case, the ECJ held that the Irish Government's support of the Irish Goods Council's campaign was sufficient to allow the body to be considered 'public' for the purposes of Art 28 EC.

In Case C-265/95, *Commission v France*, the Court went even further by declaring that the actions of French farmers, who had disrupted imports, came within the ambit of the French Government, as the State authorities were considered not to have taken sufficient action to ensure free movement.

ii. Judicial development of Art 28

The Court's jurisprudence has been responsible for developing Art 28 EC into a formidable tool in the drive against national rules which restrict the free movement of goods. In an attempt to illustrate this development, the Court's decisions will be considered in chronological order.

6. 'The *Dassonville* formula'

While Directive 70/50/EEC provided that IDAMs do not normally come within the scope of Art 28 EC, the ECJ has held in Case 8/74,

Procureur du Roi v Dassonville, that: 'All trading rules enacted by Member States which are capable of hindering directly or indirectly, actually or potentially, intra-Community trade are to be considered as measures having an effect equivalent to quantitative restrictions.'

In what has become the authoritative definition of an MHEE, the Court interpreted Art 28 EC to bring non-discriminatory as well as discriminatory measures within its scope. In *Dassonville*, the ECJ also provided that it is not necessary to show an actual effect on trade between Member States – it is sufficient to show that the measure is capable of such an effect. This is a particularly all-encompassing interpretation, allowing Member States very little scope in their trading rules.

7. *Cassis* and the 'Rule of Reason'

In Case 120/78, *Rewe-Zentral v Bundesmonopolverwaltung fur Branntwein* (the *Cassis de Dijon* case), the ECJ qualified the above approach by applying a 'Rule of Reason'. The Court held that, in the absence of Community harmonisation rules, where the measure in question is an IDAM (i.e. non-discriminatory), it may be justified and therefore not come within the scope of Art 28 EC provided that it is:

(a) 'necessary' (i.e. its aim cannot be achieved through less restrictive means: also known as *proportionality*) in order to satisfy

(b) a 'mandatory' requirement. (This term can better be understood when considering the Case C-120/95, *Decker*, where the ECJ substituted 'overriding reason in the general interest')

The Court went on to list particular areas where this may occur, in particular:

- the effectiveness of fiscal supervision;
- the protection of public health;
- the fairness of commercial transactions;
- consumer protection.

This list is not, however, exhaustive and the ECJ has shown itself willing to extend the areas which have included the promotion of national culture (Cases 60 and 61/84, *Cinéthèque v Federation des Cinemas Francais*), protection of the environment (Case 302/86, *Commission v Denmark*, the *Danish Bottles* case) and more recently, fundamental rights (CaseC-112/00, *Schmidberger v Austria*).

Prior to the introduction of the 'Rule of Reason' in *Cassis*, it was thought that all measures caught within the '*Dassonville* formula' would be prohibited by Art 28 EC unless they could be justified under Art 30 EC (discussed below). Following *Cassis*, it could be concluded that non-discriminatory measures may escape Art 28 EC, provided they can fulfil the criteria set out above. The approach taken in *Cassis* was confirmed in the Case 788/79, *Italian State v Gilli and Andres* (the *Italian Vinegar* case).

8. The distinction between 'selling arrangements' and 'product requirements': *Keck*

Due to confusion over the scope of Art 28 (and the consequent volume of cases coming before national courts and the ECJ), in Cases C-267 and 268/91, *Keck and Mithouard*, the Court took the opportunity to 're-examine and clarify' its case law relating to MHEEs.

The Court held that *'contrary to what has previously been decided . . . certain selling arrangements'* were outside the scope of the *Dassonville* formula, provided that they applied *'to all affected traders operating within the national territory and provided they affect in the same manner, in law and in fact, the marketing of domestic products and those from other Member States'*. Simplified, this means that certain past decisions of the Court can no longer be considered 'good' law and *also* that 'selling arrangements', when non-discriminatory, are outside the scope of Art 28 EC.

While the Court's judgement was intended to clarify the law, in reality, it caused some confusion, particularly with regard to:

- the exact nature of 'selling arrangements', and
- which past decisions were no longer 'good' law

The Court's judgement appears to distinguish between measures which:

(1) relate to the goods themselves, that is their intrinsic qualities or 'product requirements' such as composition, size, labelling, packaging, weight, form and so on and those measures which.

(2) relate to extrinsic matters or 'selling arrangements' such as marketing or advertising, who may sell the goods and where or when goods may be sold.

To reiterate, while *all* discriminatory measures continue to be prohibited by Art 28 EC, the Court appears to have provided that measures relating to 'product requirements', or intrinsic qualities, come within the scope of Art 28 and are prohibited, while those relating to 'selling arrangements', or extrinsic qualities, do not.

Later decisions of the ECJ appear to support this conclusion. In Cases C-401 and 402/92, *Tankstation 't vof* and *Boermans*, for example, the Court held a rule prohibiting the advertising of certain pharmaceutical products to be a 'selling arrangement' which was, as such, not prohibited by Art 28 EC. Similarly, in Case C-292/92, *Hunermund*, the Court also considered a rule relating to the compulsory closing times of petrol stations to be a 'selling arrangement' and consequently outside the scope of Art 28 EC.

i. Measures which impede or prevent market access

As has already been demonstrated, national measures which directly discriminate between domestic goods and imported goods are prohibited by Art 28 EC (*Dassonville*).

Similarly, following *Keck*, it was thought that non-discriminatory selling arrangements were outside the scope of Art 28 EC. The ECJ has, however, made it clear that national measures, which are indirectly discriminatory, or impede the market access of non-domestic goods to a greater degree than domestic goods will also come within the definition of an MHEE.

In Cases C-34 to 36/95, *De Agostini and TV Shop*, which related to a Swedish ban on advertising, aimed at young children, the ECJ provided that the national rule was prohibited by Art 28 EC as it had a greater detrimental affect on goods from other Member States, than it did on domestic goods.

Similarly in Case C-405/98, *Konsumentombudsmannen v Gourmet International Products* (the *Gourmet Foods* case), Swedish law prohibited the advertising of alcoholic beverages in trade magazines. While this rule was not directly discriminatory, being targeted at both domestic and non-domestic products, it was successfully argued that it had a far more detrimental effect on the less well known non-domestic brands than on domestic brands. It was consequently considered to be an MHEE despite, at first consideration, appearing to be a non-discriminatory 'selling arrangement' saved by the '*Keck* principle'.

ii. The present state of affairs

As can be gleaned from the above discussions, the extent of the rules contained within Art 28 EC is still not entirely certain. It would appear, however, that when considering whether a State measure comes within the

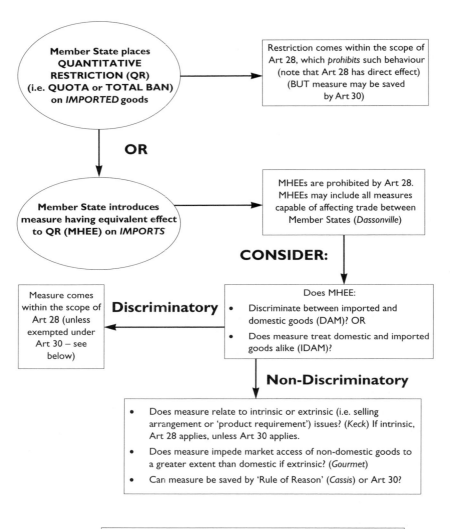

The Prohibition of Quantitative Restrictions and Measures Having Equivalent Effect on IMPORTS

scope of Art 28 EC, the following should be considered:

- Whether or not the measure is distinctly applicable (i.e. discriminatory) (*Dassonville*). If so, it is prohibited.

- If it is non-discriminatory, whether it is a 'selling arrangement' or a 'product requirement' (*Keck*). If a 'product requirement' it will be prohibited.

- If it is a 'selling arrangement', whether it prevents or impedes the market access of non-domestic goods to a greater extent than domestic goods (*De Agostini* and *Gourmet*). If yes, again the measure will be prohibited.

- Whether, even where it appears to be caught by Art 28 EC, the rule can be justified either by the 'Rule of Reason' (but *only* if non-discriminatory) (*Cassis*, discussed above) or provided with a derogation under Art 30 EC (discussed below).

9. MHEEs and exports (Art 29 EC)

There may be instances, although less frequent than in relation to imports, where a Member State may wish to restrict the free flow of exports and consequently the Community has responded to such a possibility.

Article 29 EC prohibits quantitative restrictions and all MHEEs on exported goods. While the prohibition contained within Art 29 EC *appears* to mirror that contained within Art 28 EC, this is not the case, as ECJ decisions such as *Dassonville, Cassis* and *Keck* related to the Court's interpretation of Art 28, not Art 29.

While Art 28 EC has been held to prohibit both DAMs (discriminatory measures) and IDAMs (measures which treat domestic and other goods alike), it would appear that Art 29 only prohibits measures which discriminate (DAMs) (Case 15/79, *Groenveld*).

Examples of measures that have been held to be MHEEs with regard to exports include Case 237/82, *Jongeneel Kaas v Netherlands*, where inspection documents were required for exports while no such requirement was placed on goods destined for the domestic market. See also Case C-5/94, *R v MAFF ex p Lomas*, where national authorities refused to sanction the

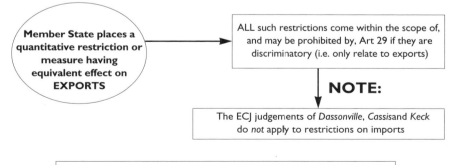

Quantitative Restrictions and MHEEs on EXPORTS

export of live animals to States where slaughterhouse standards were not thought to be adequate.

10. Derogation from the provisions of Arts 28 and 29 (Art 30 EC)

i. What the Treaty says

The Community has recognised that certain measures put into effect by Member States, although detrimental to free movement of goods, may be necessary to fulfil important functions. In order to give effect to the recognition that the positive effects of certain measures outweigh the negative effects on trade, Art 30 EC provides that: 'The provisions of Arts 28 and 29 shall not preclude prohibitions or restrictions on imports, exports or goods in transit justified on grounds of':

- public morality;
- public security or policy;
- protection of the health and life of humans, animals or plants;
- protection of national treasures;
- protection of industrial and commercial property.

The Article goes on to qualify this, providing that: 'Such prohibitions or restrictions shall not, however, constitute a means of arbitrary discrimination or a disguised restriction on trade between Member States.'

ii. The jurisprudence of the ECJ

As touched upon earlier, the ECJ has adopted a narrow stance with regard to its interpretation of the measures which may enjoy a derogation under Art 30, as to do otherwise could constitute a threat to the Community's fundamental principle of free movement of goods.

Considering first the qualifications added as a rider to Art 30 EC, the Court's attitude is best discovered by consideration of some of its decisions.

'Arbitrary discrimination'

In Case 152/78, *Commission v France*, French advertising restrictions appeared to be biased against grain-based spirits, while favouring fruit-based spirits. The French authorities attempted to justify this on the grounds of 'public health', arguing that grain-based spirits were more likely to be injurious to health. Independent evidence, however, showed the effect on health of both spirits to be identical. Interestingly, the French produce fruit-based spirits, while grain-based spirits are generally imported. The Court, in its judgement, considered the restriction to be capricious, constituting arbitrary discrimination.

'Disguised restriction on trade'

In Case 40/82, *Commission v UK*, the *Newcastle Disease* case, the United Kingdom banned the import of poultry and poultry products from countries which did not have a policy of slaughtering birds with Newcastle disease. The United Kingdom attempted to justify this on the grounds of 'health'. Evidence showed that other methods of controlling the disease were equally effective and that the ban had been imposed following pressure from UK poultry producers relating to an increase of turkeys imported from France. Furthermore, when French importers complied with UK requirements, additional restrictions were imposed. The ECJ concluded that the UK's restrictions amounted to a disguised restriction on trade.

The requirement of 'proportionality'

Although not specifically mentioned in Art 30 EC, it is implicit that the general principle of proportionality will apply to any measure for which a Member State is claiming justification. The principle requires that measures be no more than strictly necessary to achieving a particular aim (Case 124/81, *Commission v UK, Re UHT Milk*).

The grounds for justification

The Treaty provides a closed list of grounds under which a Member State may claim derogation from the prohibitions provided by Arts 28 and 29 EC. The Court has generally expressed unwillingness to consider any extension of these grounds, as it sees this as a matter for legislation (as evidenced in Case 113/80, *Commission v Ireland*, the *Irish Souvenirs* case). However, a more liberal attitude may be emerging, as demonstrated in Case C-379/98, *Preussen Elektra*, which involved derogation on the grounds of environmental protection.

11. Public morality

Consideration of Case 34/79, *R v Henn and Darby* and Case 121/85, *Conegate Ltd v HM Customs & Excise*, which are the main authorities in this area, provide examples of the Court's interpretation of this ground.

In *Henn and Darby*, the defendants were accused by UK authorities of illegally importing pornographic material. They argued, in their defence, that UK rules contravened Art 28 EC. The ECJ found that the UK's ban on pornography was justified under Art 30 EC, as it is for each Member State to determine the standards of public morality which exist within its own territory.

In Conegate, the defendants imported inflatable, life size 'love dolls' into the United Kingdom. The dolls were seized and, once more, it was argued that the UK rules constituted a threat to trade. The UK rules did not contain a similar ban on the domestic manufacture of 'love dolls' and, although the Court repeated its dicta from *Henn and Darby*, it was held that a Member State may not rely on Art 30 EC 'when its legislation contains no prohibition on the manufacture or marketing of the same goods in its territory'.

What can be concluded from these decisions is that while the Member States are free to determine moral standards within their own States, they must not place any stricter burden on non-domestic goods than they do on nationally produced goods.

12. Public policy

Case 7/78, *R v Thompson and Others* – a rare example of a successful action under this ground – involved the right to mint (and melt down) coinage. The Court held that this ground could be successful where there is a need to protect a right that is traditionally regarded as involving a fundamental interest of the State.

13. Public security

This ground often goes hand in hand with a claim based on public policy. In Case 72/83, *Campus Oil Ltd v Minister for Industry and Energy*, importers of petroleum products were required to buy 35 per cent of their oil from the Irish National Petroleum Company at a fixed price. The ECJ accepted that this was to enable the Irish Government to maintain a viable refinery that could meet essential needs in times of crisis and that the national measure could be justified as in the interests of public security.

14. Protection of health and life of humans, animals or plants

The ECJ has made it clear that when considering whether or not a measure may be justified under this ground, there are a number of issues which may be relevant to its deliberations. These have been held to include the following:

(a) the presence, or otherwise, of harmonising legislation. In the absence of harmonising legislation, the principle of 'mutual recognition' may be relevant. This principle is discussed in further detail below but, briefly, it provides that goods lawfully produced in one Member State should be presumed to reach minimum requirement standards in all Member States (Case 190/87, *Oberkreisdirektor v Moorman*);

(b) the state of scientific knowledge (Case 174/82, *Officier van Justitie v Sandoz* and Case 178/84, *Commission v Germany*, the *German Beer* case). Where it is undecided, the Member State will be provided with a degree of discretion, bearing in mind:

- the principle of proportionality (*Sandoz* and the *UHT Milk* case);
- the existence of a technical need (*German Beer* case) – this is often particularly relevant with regard to rules relating to additives;
- the true need for inspections/spot checks (again, the rule of 'mutual recognition' may be relevant). In Case 4/75, *Rewe-Zentralfinanz v Landschwirtschaftskammer* (*San José Scale*), it was held that inspections will only be justified if imported products constitute a real risk not present in comparable domestic goods, while in Case 228/91, *Commission v Italy*, the Court provided that where health certificates are available, spot checks, rather than continual inspection, will be judged as necessary on imports.

It should be evident that an overlap exists between measures justifiable under the 'Rule of Reason' (*Cassis*) and Art 30 EC, particularly in the area of 'public health'. However, when Member States have previously sought to justify measures on public health grounds, the Court has chosen to consider such requests under Art 30.

15. Protection of national treasures

There is a paucity of definitive case law in this area and therefore little guidance as to what will be considered to be a 'national treasure'. In the *1st Art Treasures* case, which was brought as a result of Italy's breach of Art 25 EC, the ECJ failed to allow the Italian Government to levy an export tax on 'cultural artefacts' in an attempt to restrict their removal abroad. While Italy's actions were prohibited, the Court's judgement added little to academic understanding in relation to this ground.

16. Protection of industrial or commercial property

Industrial or commercial property (also known as 'intellectual property') rights may take the form of trade marks, copyright, patents and so on. Protection of such rights encourages innovation and their ownership is complemented by Art 295 EC, which provides that: 'The Treaty shall in no way prejudice the rules in Member States governing the system of property ownership.'

Where national rules allow such rights to be protected, an individual with an intellectual property right (IPR) can often rely on such legislation to prevent reimportation of particular goods. National legislation relating to an IPR may, however, have the result of restricting trade which is, of course, prohibited under Community law.

The ECJ has struck a balance between the necessary protection of an IPR and the principle of free movement of goods by distinguishing between the existence of an IPR and the exercise of such rights. The Court has provided that an IPR will be protected by Art 30 EC, only when rights have not been exhausted by the subject matter of the right being put into free circulation within the Community (Case 15/74, *Centrafarm v Sterling Drug*). This is probably best understood by the provision of the following example.

An inventor (A) has patented a new invention and so an IPR exists. Should A decide to award a licence to manufacturer B, giving B the right to produce the invention, A will be said to have exercised his IP rights.

If the product remains within the Member State, the rights afforded by the award of a patent will be subject to the intellectual property laws of that Member State only and Community rules will be irrelevant.

If, however, the product is exported by B, A will not be able to exert any further control over the product, even if it is reimported, as the Community provides that his rights were exhausted or 'used up' when he awarded B authority over the product.

The doctrine of exhaustion of rights has been held to be applicable to:

- patents – Case 15/74, Centrafarm v Sterling Drug;
- trade marks – Case 16/74, Centrafarm v Winthrop;
- copyright – Case 78/70, Deutsche Grammophon v Metro.

It should be noted that a certain amount of secondary legislation has been adopted by the Community with the aim of harmonising the rules in this area and such legislation, although outside the scope of this book, should always be considered.

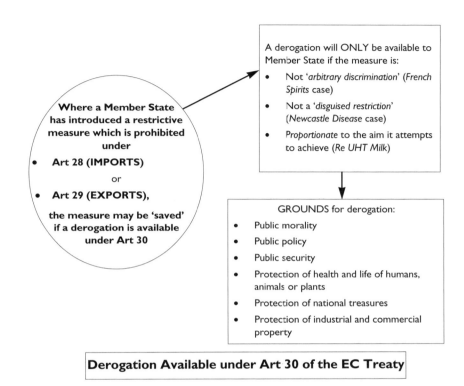

A derogation will ONLY be available to Member State if the measure is:

- Not 'arbitrary discrimination' (French Spirits case)
- Not a 'disguised restriction' (Newcastle Disease case)
- Proportionate to the aim it attempts to achieve (Re UHT Milk)

Where a Member State has introduced a restrictive measure which is prohibited under

- **Art 28 (IMPORTS)**

or

- **Art 29 (EXPORTS),**

the measure may be 'saved' if a derogation is available under Art 30

GROUNDS for derogation:

- Public morality
- Public policy
- Public security
- Protection of health and life of humans, animals or plants
- Protection of national treasures
- Protection of industrial and commercial property

Derogation Available under Art 30 of the EC Treaty

i. Non-pecuniary barriers to trade and harmonisation of trading rules:

The principle of 'mutual recognition' (the 'Second Cassis Principle')

In *Cassis*, the ECJ developed a second highly important principle. The Court provided that, in the absence of harmonising legislation, there should be a presumption by Member States that goods which have been lawfully produced and marketed in one Member State will comply with the minimum requirements of the importing State.

The presumption can however be *rebutted* by evidence that further measures are necessary to ensure adequate standards are met (Case 18/84, *Commission v France*).

The principle has also been important to the process of harmonisation of trading rules within the Community. In order to create an integrated market, the Community recognises that trading rules within the Member

States must be in harmony with one another and the Commission has since provided that: *'Any product imported from another Member State must in principle be admitted to the territory of the importing Member State if it has been lawfully produced, that is, conforms to rules and processes of manufacture that are customarily and traditionally accepted in the exporting country, and is marketed in the territory of another.'* (Commission Communication OJ 1980 256/2.)

III. CONCLUSIONS

Students who have made it this far will probably agree with a comment made at the beginning of this chapter, that is, the rules relating to the free movement of goods are complex! In recognition of this fact, a flow chart is provided below in order to assist students navigate the shark-infested waters often encountered when attempting to answer questions in this area.

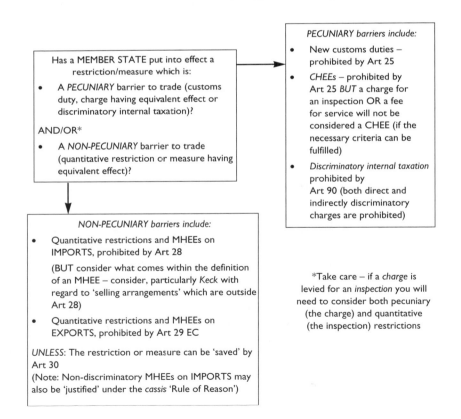

8 Free Movement of Persons and Services

As already considered, economic integration of the Member States is a primary aim of the EC (Art 2 EC). In order to ensure that this aim is achieved, the EC Treaty provides that all obstacles to the free movement of goods, persons, services and capital be abolished within the Community (Arts 3 and 14 EC).

Free movement of persons is considered to be fundamental to the creation of the common market. Without a mobile workforce, British workers, for example, would not be able to move to Germany to provide their labour should a manpower or skills shortage exist there. Similarly, a Belgian entrepreneur would not be able to expand her business into France, nor a Swedish physiotherapist cross the border into Denmark to provide his occasional services to a client with back problems!

The consequences of such occurrences would be detrimental to the creation of an integrated Community. Unsurprisingly therefore, the EC Treaty gives the *right* to all Union citizens to move from their home State to another EC State, in order to work, set up a business or provide a service, largely unhampered by frontier controls and discrimination based on their nationality. Articles 39–55 EC provide a framework of rights, which have been expanded by secondary legislation and developed by the jurisprudence of the ECJ. Community law also provides Member States with a number of *obligations* relating to the treatment of EU citizens who move from state to state within the Community.

The provision of rights of free movement within the Community does not, of course, only have economic implications and the social aspects of such rights are also important. Indeed, the concept of free movement of persons has changed significantly over the years. Originally seen as factors of production in the same way as, for example, raw materials, persons – in their relatively new guise as European citizens – are now given rights independent of their economic status.

In addition to providing rights of free movement, the EU has attempted to abolish checks at internal borders and all Member States, other than the United Kingdom and Ireland, have now signed the Schengen agreement on this. In reality, however, the variety of languages spoken within the Community undoubtedly has an adverse effect on cross-border mobility. Tethered largely by linguistic differences, it is interesting to note that less than 1 per cent of EU citizens live outside their country of origin.

I. THE IMPORTANCE OF CITIZENSHIP OF THE EU

It is essential to understand at the outset that rights relating to free movement are only *directly* provided to citizens of the EU. This is demonstrated by Art 18 EC, which provides that: 'Every citizen of the Union shall have the right to move and reside freely within the territory of the Member States.'

Who then is to be considered a 'citizen of the Union'? Introduced by the ToA in an attempt to strengthen ties between the EU and its citizens, Art 17 EC established the concept of Union citizenship and provides that: 'Every person holding the nationality of a Member State shall be a citizen of the Union.' Consequently, only those holding the nationality of one of the Member States have direct access to rights and benefits relating to free movement.

This does not mean that nationals of third countries have no rights under Community law. Indeed, non-EU family members of Union citizens will, for example, normally enjoy rights indirectly via their relationship to the EU citizen, while Arts 61–69 EC, which relate to issues such as visas, immigration and asylum, also provide and safeguard the rights of non-EU nationals. As yet, however, no coherent body of rules govern the treatment of third country nationals through out the Community.

II. THE RELEVANCE OF 'ECONOMIC STATUS'

Once it has been established that a person wishing to enjoy rights of free movement is a citizen of the EU, in order to clarify the exact nature and, importantly, the source of their rights, it is necessary to determine their 'status'. This is because Community law differentiates between different categories of EU citizen, with the Treaty largely concentrating on the provision of rights for those who are economically active and secondary legislation normally providing rights to those who are non-economically active.

1. Free movement of 'non-economically active' persons

It is understandable that the Treaty is largely silent on the rights of those who are not economically active, as the activities of the Community are largely – and traditionally – economic in nature. Initially, three directives (often known as the '90s Directives') provided non-economically active Union citizens – namely students, retirees (either through age or ill-health) and those with sufficient resources not to become a burden on the social security system of the host State – with rights of free movement and residence comparable to those enjoyed by workers and other economically active groups.

In April 2006 new legislation, in the form of Directive 2004/38, on the rights of EU citizens and their families to move and reside freely within the EU, was introduced. It repealed the earlier legislation and it is now this directive which largely provides the detailed rules by which Union citizens may move to, and stay in, a host State.

2. Free movement for those who are 'economically active'

The Treaty differentiates between categories of economic activity, namely:

- employment/workers' rights: Arts 39–42 EC relate to the rights of wage and salary earners to take up employment – and permanent residence – in a host State;
- self employment/establishment: Arts 43–48 EC relate to the rights of the self-employed and businesses to establish a permanent base in a host State;
- services: Arts 49–55 EC relate to the right to enter a host State in order to provide services on a *temporary* basis.

In addition to the above, the Treaty also contains certain, less specific provisions which underpin the free movement of persons. These include

OVERVIEW OF FREE MOVEMENT OF PERSONS

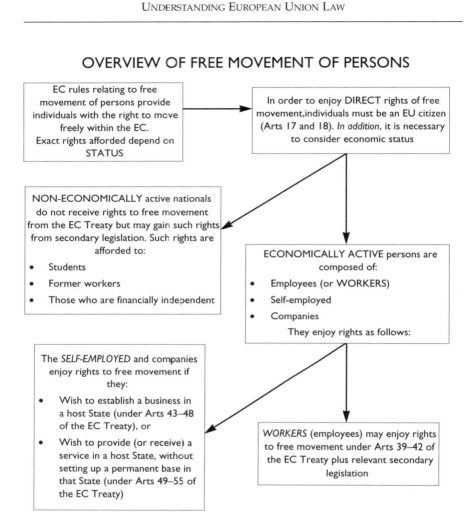

EC rules relating to free movement of persons provide individuals with the right to move freely within the EC. Exact rights afforded depend on STATUS

In order to enjoy DIRECT rights of free movement, individuals must be an EU citizen (Arts 17 and 18). *In addition*, it is necessary to consider economic status

NON-ECONOMICALLY active nationals do not receive rights to free movement from the EC Treaty but may gain such rights from secondary legislation. Such rights are afforded to:

- Students
- Former workers
- Those who are financially independent

ECONOMICALLY ACTIVE persons are composed of:

- Employees (or WORKERS)
- Self-employed
- Companies

They enjoy rights as follows:

The *SELF-EMPLOYED* and companies enjoy rights to free movement if they:

- Wish to establish a business in a host State (under Arts 43–48 of the EC Treaty), or
- Wish to provide (or receive) a service in a host State, without setting up a permanent base in that State (under Arts 49–55 of the EC Treaty)

WORKERS (employees) may enjoy rights to free movement under Arts 39–42 of the EC Treaty plus relevant secondary legislation

Art 12 EC, which provides a general prohibition on discrimination on the grounds of nationality.

III. FREE MOVEMENT OF WORKERS (ARTS 39–42 EC)

As explained above, Treaty provisions have been expanded by secondary legislation and both the primary and secondary legislation has been subject to extensive interpretation by the ECJ. Each of these sources of Community law will be considered in turn.

1. How is the term 'worker' defined?

Neither the Treaty nor secondary legislation provides a definition of the term 'worker'. The ECJ has made it clear, however, that as it is a Community concept, the Court alone has jurisdiction to define the term. While case law makes it clear that 'worker' generally refers to an employed person, the term has been interpreted very widely, allowing as many citizens as possible to enjoy the rights provided – and thus promoting free movement.

The following decisions provide a flavour of the Court's broad and inclusive interpretation of 'worker':

- Case 75/63, *Hoekstra (née Unger) v BBDA* – a worker who had lost his job but was capable of finding another should be considered a worker;

- Case 53/81, *Levin v Staatssecretaris* – a part time employee is to be considered a worker, provided the work is 'real' or genuine work of an economic nature and not nominal or minimal;

- Case 139/85, *Kempf v Staatssecretaris van Justitie* – a part time music teacher (from Germany), even though in receipt of supplementary benefit (in the Netherlands) to bring his wage up to minimum levels, came within the term;

- Case 196/87, *Steymann v Staatssecretaris van Justitie* – a member of a religious community provided with his 'keep' and pocket money, but not formal wages, was held to be a worker;

- Case 344/87, *Bettray v Staatssecretaris van Justitie* – an important case demonstrating the limits of the term 'worker'. It was held that, as the position was artificially created by the Government as part of a drug rehabilitation programme, he could not be considered to be engaged in 'economic activity' of a 'genuine' nature.

- Case C-292/89, *R v Immigration Appeal Tribunal ex p Antonissen* – although not directly relating to the definition of 'worker', provides that an individual with a genuine chance of finding work should be allowed to enter and remain for a reasonable amount of time while seeking work. This has now been confirmed by Art 14 and developed by Art 6 of the directive, which provides that any Union citizen may reside in a host state for up to three months without the usual formalities, providing they have a passport or a valid identity card. (The rights of those searching for work are not, however, as extensive as those of worker, Art 14).

2. Rights of exit, entry and residence afforded to workers

Article 39 EC contains the principal provisions relating to migrant workers. These include:

- the right to accept offers of employment actually made and to move freely within the host State for this purpose;
- the right to reside in the host State, for the purpose of employment, under the same rules as enjoyed by nationals; and
- the right to remain in the host State after having been employed in that State (following retirement or incapacity).

i. What does secondary legislation say?

The rights provided by the Treaty have been extended and expanded by secondary legislation. Arts 4 and 5 of Directive 2004/38 EC relate to rights concerned with exiting a home State and entering a host State.

In order to ensure that a home State cannot deny exit to key workers, Art 4 provides that nationals must be provided with a passport or identity card, while the directive further provides that a host State cannot create a barrier to free movement by making it prohibitively difficult for migrant workers to enter a host State, by demanding entry visas or other such documents (Art 5).

While all EU citizen have the right to reside in a host State for up to three months, a worker will have the right to reside after this period, although this may be subject to a requirement to register with the relevant authorities of the host State (Art 8). The right of permanent residency becomes available to those who have legally resided for a continuous period of five years in the host State. (Generally, a period will be continuous provided that any absences are limited to no more than six months out of every year. The right may be lost if there is a continuous absence of over two years.)

3. The right to be treated equally with domestic workers

Once installed in a host State, Art 39 EC provides that migrant workers must not be discriminated against on the basis of their nationality, in terms of their employment, remuneration and other conditions of work and employment. This is supported by Art 12 EC, which provides a more general right not to be discriminated against on the basis of nationality.

i. What does secondary legislation say?

Arts 7–9 of Regulation 1612/68 EEC reiterate and expand upon equality in employment, although the legislation recognises that conditions relating to linguistic knowledge, required by reason of the nature of the post to be filled, may be permitted (Art 3). Both direct and covert discrimination is outlawed, with workers being provided with equality in regard to areas such as access to vocational training and housing. Art 7 is particularly relevant, as it provides that the same 'social advantages' be made available to migrant workers, as are enjoyed by nationals – which takes equality outside the scope of employment alone.

This theme is taken up by Art 24 of Directive 2004/38 EC, which provides that workers should normally enjoy 'equal treatment with nationals', which again supports the idea of equality *outside* employment, as well as within.

IV. THE APPROACH OF THE ECJ

The case law of the ECJ interprets not only the Treaty but also secondary legislation. While the bulk of secondary legislation on the free movement of persons within the EU was repealed in April 2006, it is likely that the case law will still remain relevant to Directive 2004/38, as the new legislation is largely consolidating in nature.

1. Social advantages

The Court has, on numerous occasions, been called upon to clarify the situation with regard to the extent of the 'social advantages' to be enjoyed by migrant workers. The ECJ has made it clear that the term should not be interpreted restrictively.

In Case 207/78, *Ministère Public v Even* and *ONPTS*, the ECJ provided guidance as to the factors that should be taken into account when determining what rights amount to 'social advantages'. The Court explained that (1) status as a worker (2) residence in the host State and (3) the likelihood of the benefit accruing from the 'advantage' facilitating mobility within the Community, were relevant considerations although, in practice, this test has often been found to be inconclusive.

An interesting case which demonstrates the extent of 'social advantage' is Case 59/85, *Netherlands v Reed*. Here, the ECJ provided that an unmarried, migrant worker may enjoy the presence of his/her partner (who fails to have rights of entry and residence independently) as a 'social advantage' provided that, under domestic law, married and unmarried partners enjoy the same rights in that State. This approach has now been incorporated into the new directive, which provides that a 'partner with whom the Union citizen has a durable relationship' shall benefit from rights under the Directive (Art 3).

The right to claim equal social advantages was, however, subject to a limitation in Case 316/85, *Centre Public de l'Aide Social de Courcelles v Lebon*. In this case, it was held that equality of treatment in respect of all social advantages was only available to persons entitled to reside by reason of employment, and not to persons permitted temporary rights of residence in order to *search* for work.

2. Linguistic knowledge

While Regulation 1612/68 permits the application of conditions relating to linguistic knowledge, the ECJ, in Case 379/87, *Groener v Minister of Education*, explained that State policy regarding linguistic knowledge must not be disproportionate to the aim to be achieved, nor should the manner in which it is applied discriminate against migrant workers. *Groener*, a Dutch national, was not appointed to a teaching post at an Irish college when she failed an oral test. The test, which related to her competency in Gaelic, applied to both nationals and migrant workers alike, had been introduced to encourage the use of the language and was held to be valid.

3. The extent of 'discrimination'

i. Indirect discrimination

While Community rules obviously prohibit direct discrimination on grounds of nationality, the ECJ has also outlawed indirect discrimination, that is, the imposition of national rules that are *more easily satisfied* by nationals than by migrant workers. In Case C-237/94, *O'Flynn v Adjudication Officer*, for example, the ECJ was prepared to recognise that an apparently neutral UK rule which allowed workers to claim burial grants, only when the burial was held in the United Kingdom, was indirectly discriminatory and consequently contrary to Community law. (This can be compared to the manner in which the Court has declared that both distinctly and indistinctly applicable measures may be prohibited under rules relating to the free movement of goods (Chapter 7)).

ii. Access to the employment market

The ECJ has been prepared to go beyond merely prohibiting measures that discriminate – either directly or indirectly – between domestic and migrant workers.

In Case C-415/93, *Union Royale Belge des Sociétés de Football Association ASBL v Bosman* (the *Bosman* case), the ECJ explained that measures which restrict the freedom of movement of workers are prohibited *despite* not discriminating on grounds of nationality. In *Bosman*, the transnational transfer system relating to footballers was held to be an excessive obstacle to free movement, as it was capable of preventing players from obtaining employment in other Member States. However, it was also explained that such restrictive measures *may* be objectively justified by a Member State on public interest grounds.

iii Justification of indirect discrimination and restrictive measures

It should be noted that indirect discrimination may be subject to objective justification by the host State (e.g. Case 279/93, *Schumacker*, and Case 204/90, *Bachmann*, relating to tax rules), while direct discrimination may not.

Although first developed in relation to the free movement of services (Case 33/74, *Van Binsbergen*, and Case 279/80, *Webb*), the Court has also provided that where a national measure hinders free movement rather than discriminates against non-nationals, that measure may be justified in appropriate circumstances (*Bosman*).

In Case C-55/94, *Gebhard*, the ECJ provided that 'national measures liable to hinder or make less attractive the exercise of fundamental freedoms guaranteed by the Treaty must fulfil four conditions', if they are not to fall foul of Community law. The Court then went on to list these conditions as follows:

- the rules must be applied in a non-discriminatory manner;
- they must be justified by imperative requirements in the general interest;
- they must be suitable for securing the attainment of the objective which they pursue;
- they must not go beyond what is necessary to attain it (proportionality).

This approach can be compared to the Court's approach in relation to free movement of goods. In *Cassis*, the ECJ developed the 'Rule of Reason', which provides circumstances in which a restrictive measure could be justified. It can be argued that the ECJ's jurisprudence in both areas is developing along somewhat similar lines.

4. The right of migrant workers to remain in a host State after employment has ceased

Article 39(3)(d) EC provides workers with the right to remain in a host State after being employed in that State.

The right of a worker to remain in a host State on retirement or where s/he ceases to be employed as a result of permanent incapacity, is now expanded upon by Art 17 Directive 2004/38. While the right of permanent residence is provided, by Art 16, to all workers who have been resident for a continuous *Five year* period (discussed above), those who reach the retirement age of the host State after:

- working in that State for at least the preceding 12 months of their retirement *and*
- have resided there continuously for at least three years,

will also enjoy the same rights of permanent residence.

Similarly, those who are permanently incapacitated, as a result of an industrial accident or occupational disease, will enjoy permanent rights of residence immaterial of how long they have resided in that State. Those who are incapacitated by other illnesses will, however, be required to have completed at least two years continuous residence in order to be entitled to reside permanently.

5. Workers who live in one host State but work in another

Certain workers may find themselves working in one host State while residing in another. Providing such workers can demonstrate:

- three years' continuous residence and employment in the territory of a host State where they wish to remain; and
- they return at least once a week to that State,

they will have the right of permanent residency in the State in which they are domiciled, after ceasing work in the second host State (Art 17).

6. Rights relating to workers' families

Primary legislation does not directly refer to a migrant worker's right to be joined by his/her family, nor does it specify what entitlements family members may enjoy in a host State. This has been left to secondary legislation and Directive 2004/38 now provides rights in relation to workers' families.

i. The composition of a worker's 'family'

Arts 2 and 3, Directive 2004/38 provide that a 'family member', irrespective of nationality, may be:

- a spouse;
- a partner with whom the worker has entered into a registered partnership, *providing* that the host State recognises such partnerships are equivalent to marriage;
- a direct descendant under 21, or dependant of the worker or his/her spouse or partner;
- a direct ascendant, provided they are dependent on the worker, spouse or partner;
- any other dependant family member, who in the 'home' State was resident in the household *or* who has serious health problems requiring personal care;
- a partner with whom the worker has a durable relationship. (Note that it is for the host State to investigate this and to justify any denial of entry or residence.)

(The term 'spouse' has been restrictively interpreted by the Court to include legally married persons only (Case 59/85, *Reed*). However, in that case, the Court went on to explain that in a Member State where a stable relationship enjoyed by an unmarried couple is accorded similar status to marriage, this will be considered to be a 'social advantage', as to treat such couples differently would amount to discrimination. It would appear that this interpretation of the legislation has now been incorporated into the new directive by virtue of Art 3.)

ii. Rights to be enjoyed by workers' families

Where family members are citizens of one of the EU Member States, both the Treaty (Art 18) and secondary legislation (Directive 2004/38) make it clear that a general right of free movement is available to them as Union citizens – subject to certain restrictions (which are considered below).

In addition, family members who are nationals of countries outside the EU also have rights of free movement, albeit indirect, as a result of their relationship with the worker.

Family rights of exit, entry and residence

Directive 2004/39 provides that family members, who are EU citizens, enjoy the same rights of exit and entry as the worker. Where a family member is not an EU citizen, again rights are very similar, other than they may be required to provide an entry visa or valid residence card (Art 5).

As mentioned above, all Union citizens have a right of residence in a host State for up to three months. This right is also extended to family members who are non-EU citizens (Art 6).

Similarly, family members, irrespective of their nationality and by virtue of their relationship to the worker, will be afforded the right of residence for more than three months on the same basis as the worker (Art 7, discussed above). In the case of non-EU citizens, this is subject to the issue of a residence card, which should be issued expediently by the host State, on production of certain documentation (listed in Art 10 of Directive 2004/38).

Once family members have been legally resident in the host State for a continuous period of five years, they will, under the same conditions as the worker (again, as discussed above), have the right of permanent residence in the host State (Arts 16 and 17, Art 18 for non-EU nationals).

The right to take up employment

If the family member is a EU citizen, the right to take up employment is provided by Art 39 EC. Taking up employment in the host State will, of course, give the family member independent rights and, consequently, they will no longer need to depend on rights provided through their relationship with the original worker.

Art 23 of Directive 2004/38 reiterates this and also extends the right to non-EU family members who have rights of residence.

The right to education

Under Art 12 of Regulation 1612/68, children of a worker residing in a host State enjoy non-discriminatory access to general educational, apprenticeship and vocational training schemes. This has been broadly interpreted by the ECJ, which has held that migrant workers' children are entitled to exactly the same benefits as children of domestic workers, including educational grants (Case 76/72, *Michel S*) and it would appear that the exception to this – contained in Art 24 of Directive 2004/38 – has been interpreted by the ECJ in a manner which appears to have negated it (Case C-209/03, *R v London Borough of Ealing & Sec., Do State for Education ex parte Bidar*, where, Bidar, a French national resident with his grandmother in the United Kingdom, failed to meet the residence requirement of three years, in order to obtain a grant. It was argued that, as a EU citizen, he should be entitled to a grant on the same terms as UK citizens, a proposition with which the ECJ agreed).

The broad interpretative approach of the ECJ can also be evidenced by decisions such as Cases 389 and 390/87, *Echternach* and *Moritz v Netherlands Ministry for Education and Science*, where the Court held that children of migrant workers could remain in the host State to finish their education, even when their parents had returned home. Similarly, in Case C-7/94, *Gaal*, the Court provided that educational rights include the right to complete a course, even after a once dependent child reaches the age of 21, as to act otherwise would discourage integration.

It is not clear whether workers' spouses/partners enjoy such wide rights in relation to education, but they have been held to be entitled to equal access to educational, apprenticeship or vocational training schemes by reason of non-discrimination provisions enshrined in Art 12 EC (for example, Case 152/82, *Forcheri v Belgium*). Such rights would now appear to have been further strengthened by the requirement in Art 24 of Directive 2004/38 that workers and their family members, whether EU nationals or not, should be treated equally with nationals.

The right to remain: death or divorce

Directive 2004/38 not only details the rights of workers to remain in a host State, but also provides that the residence rights of a worker's family will normally remain unchanged if the worker dies or leaves the host State, although the right to remain of family members who are non-EU citizens, will be reliant on their having resided with the worker, in the host State, for at least 12 months prior to the worker's death (Art 12). The ECJ has also confirmed that the surviving family of a deceased worker will enjoy equality of treatment with nationals of that State (Case 32/75, *Cristini v SNCF*).

Divorce, annulment or termination of a registered partnership should also not affect the right of family members to reside (Art 13), although conditions relating to the length of the relationship, custody of children and so on, may apply where the spouse/partner is a non-EU citizen.

Other rights relating to family members

As has already been established, the rights afforded to workers' families often flow from their relationship with a migrant worker. It should also be remembered that Art 12 EC provides *all* EU citizens with a general right not to be discriminated against on grounds of their nationality, while Art 24 of Directive 2204/38 extends this right to family members who are non-EU citizens.

More specifically, the ECJ has elaborated on the extent of dependent rights in a number of cases, particularly with regard to 'social advantages'. In Case 32/75, *Cristini v SNCF*, the Court held that the right 'cannot be interpreted restrictively', as to do so would hamper integration.

V. LIMITATIONS ON THE RIGHTS OF WORKERS AND THEIR FAMILIES

1. Derogation on grounds of public policy, public security and public health: restrictions on exit, entry and residence

The Community recognises that there are certain circumstances under which it is neither reasonable nor desirable to allow workers – or their families – the right to move freely around the Community. Community law therefore provides that the Member States may deny rights in certain circumstances.

Article 39(3) EC provides that the Member States may deny workers the right of free movement on the grounds of public policy, public security or public health (it should be noted that the grounds of public policy and public security overlap to such an extent that they can, in practice, normally be regarded as a single category).

2. Secondary legislation

The derogation provided by Art 39(3) EC is repeated, and expanded upon, by Art 27 of Directive 2004/38 EC. The directive provides that measures taken on the basis of public security, public policy or public health must not be invoked to serve economic ends.

Measures taken on grounds of public policy or security must also comply with the principle of proportionality and be based exclusively on the personal conduct of the individual concerned. It is also provided that the existence of previous criminal convictions will not *automatically* allow a Member State to deny a worker his rights of entry and residence.

The directive further provides that the personal conduct of the individual concerned must present a (1) genuine, (2) present and (3) sufficiently serious threat, affecting one of the fundamental interests of the State, while it is prescribed that prohibitions which are *general* in nature shall not be accepted.

In order to ascertain whether an individual presents such a threat, when issuing a registration certificate or, in the absence of a registration system, no later than three months after the entry of the individual into a host State, or when issuing a residence card, a host State may, if it is considered essential, request that the home State provide information relating to the previous police record of the individual. A home State is required to provide an answer within two months.

Should a host State expel an individual on grounds of public policy, public security or public health, the home State which issued the passport of the individual concerned must allow the individual to re-enter its territory.

3. Protection against expulsion

Art 28 of Directive 2004/38 provides what considerations a host State should take into account before taking the decision to expel. These include the following:

- length of residence in the host State
- age
- State of health
- family
- economic situation
- social and cultural integration into the host State
- links with country of origin.

It is also provided that, where the individual has a right of permanent residence in a host State, the decision to expel should only be taken on *serious* grounds of public policy and/or security. Where the individual is a EU citizen who has:

• resided in the host State for 10 years, or

• is a minor (unless in the best interests of the child),

the decision to expel should only be taken on *imperative* grounds of public security.

In addition, the directive provides that any decision to expel must normally be provided in full and in writing (Art 30) and that there must be an appeal process in place (Art 31). Those excluded may also submit an application to have the expulsion order lifted, after a reasonable period, which should be no longer than five years (Art 32).

4. The approach of the ECJ to restrictions on exit, entry and residence

The ECJ has taken a narrow approach to the interpretation of the legislation restricting the free movement of workers. As with the exceptions to the rules governing free movement of goods (Art 30 EC), exceptions to the free movement of workers must be proportionate and objectively justifiable. The case law outlined below precedes Directive 2004/38 but is likely to still be relevant, as it can be seen that the decisions of the ECJ have now been incorporated into secondary legislation.

1. In Case 36/75, *Rutili v Ministre de l'Interieur*, the ECJ provided that a Member State claiming derogation on the grounds of public policy and/or security may only deny a worker his rights if his presence constitutes a 'genuine and sufficiently serious threat to public policy'.

2. This was extended in Case 30/77, *R v Bouchereau*, where the Court provided that the threat must also 'affect one of the fundamental interests of the State'.

3. In Cases 115 and 116/81, *Adoui* and *Cornuaille v Belgian State* (the *French Prostitutes* case), the ECJ held that derogation on grounds of public policy does not allow expulsion of a migrant worker where similar conduct by a national would not incur a proportionately restrictive sanction. (In *Adoui*, French nationals were denied entry to Belgium due to their 'moral standards', despite the fact that prostitution is not illegal there – an obvious example of discrimination against migrants.)

The dicta of the ECJ supports secondary legislation by providing that criminal convictions do not provide grounds for exclusion *unless* they provide evidence of a present threat, as can be demonstrated by the following cases:

4. Case 30/77, *R v Bouchereau*, where B, a French national, came to work in the United Kingdom in 1975. He was convicted of unlawful possession of drugs in June 1976, having pleaded guilty to a similar offence in January 1976 (for which he received a 12 month conditional discharge). The magistrates' court made a reference to the ECJ, questioning the extent to which previous convictions may be considered as a ground for exclusion. The ECJ held that previous criminal convictions may only be taken into account as evidence of personal conduct where it constitutes a present threat to the requirements of public policy, by indicating a likelihood of recurrence. Past conduct alone may, however, be sufficient to constitute a present threat if the conduct can be considered to be sufficiently serious;

5. Case 67/74, *Bonsignore v Oberstadtdirektor of the City of Cologne*, in which B, an Italian working in Germany, accidentally shot his brother. He was convicted of unlawful possession of a firearm and was ordered to be deported. He challenged the deportation order and the German courts made a reference to the ECJ, questioning whether deportation may be justified on public policy grounds as a general preventative measure to deter others. The ECJ held that the public policy requirement may only be invoked to justify a deportation for breaches of the peace and public security which may be committed by the individual concerned and not for reasons of a general preventative nature.

5. The 'public health' limitation

As touched on above, Article 39(3) EC also provides that the Member States may deny workers the right of free movement on grounds of public health.

Art 29 of Directive 2004/38 expands upon this by outlining the diseases for which expulsion is allowed but also providing that diseases which occur after three months of entry into a host State will not constitute grounds for expulsion.

6. The 'public service' exception to rights of workers

Article 39(4) EC provides that provisions of Art 39 'shall not apply to employment in the public service'.

The exact scope of 'public service' is not defined by legislation and, not surprisingly as it provides an exception to the fundamental Community principle of free movement, the concept has been narrowly interpreted by the ECJ. The Court has shed considerable light on the extent and application of the rule and the following cases are particularly enlightening.

First, the Court has held that the Art 39(4) EC cannot be invoked by the Member States in relation to the terms and conditions of employment as it applies only to *access* to employment (Case 152/73, *Sotgui v Deutsche Bundespost*).

In Case 149/79, *Commission v Belgium* (*Re Public Employees*), Belgian law reserving posts in the public service for Belgian nationals, irrespective of the duties performed, was found to come outside the scope of the Art 39(4) EC. To come within the ambit of Art 39(4), the Court held that employment must involve 'direct or indirect participation in the exercise of powers conferred by public law and duties designed to safeguard the general interests of the State or other public authorities'.

The implication of this and other supporting decisions is that posts in which the post-holder owes a particular allegiance to the State may be included (e.g. the armed forces, police, judiciary, tax authorities and high-ranking civil servants, etc). This view is reinforced by the Notice in 1988 (OJ No 72/2), in which the Commission provided some guidance as to which post would be covered. The Commission concluded that the following would be unlikely to be covered:

- public health services;
- teaching in State educational establishments;
- research for non-military purposes in public establishments;
- public bodies responsible for administering commercial services.

In view of the Court's restrictive attitude and Commission guidance, this has remained a contentious area. While the EC recognises a need for the Member States to preserve their own national identity, the Community has not been prepared to allow them to do this to the detriment of free movement.

VI. ENFORCEMENT OF RIGHTS IN RELATION TO FREE MOVEMENT OF WORKERS

In addition to understanding that Community law provides individuals with rights in relation to free movement throughout the Member States, it is also necessary to consider how such rights may be enforced and against whom.

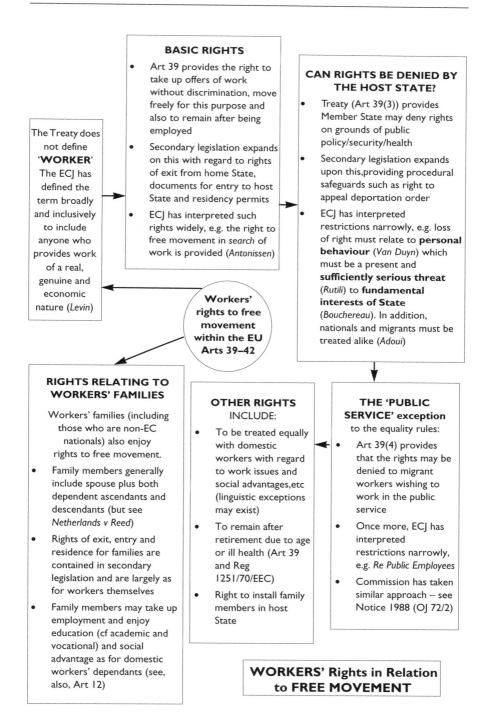

BASIC RIGHTS

- Art 39 provides the right to take up offers of work without discrimination, move freely for this purpose and also to remain after being employed

- Secondary legislation expands on this with regard to rights of exit from home State, documents for entry to host State and residency permits

- ECJ has interpreted such rights widely, e.g. the right to free movement in *search* of work is provided (*Antonissen*)

CAN RIGHTS BE DENIED BY THE HOST STATE?

- Treaty (Art 39(3)) provides Member State may deny rights on grounds of public policy/security/health

- Secondary legislation expands upon this, providing procedural safeguards such as right to appeal deportation order

- ECJ has interpreted restrictions narrowly, e.g. loss of right must relate to **personal behaviour** (*Van Duyn*) which must be a present and **sufficiently serious threat** (*Rutili*) to **fundamental interests of State** (*Bouchereau*). In addition, nationals and migrants must be treated alike (*Adoui*)

The Treaty does not define **'WORKER'** The ECJ has defined the term broadly and inclusively to include anyone who provides work of a real, genuine and economic nature (*Levin*)

Workers' rights to free movement within the EU Arts 39–42

RIGHTS RELATING TO WORKERS' FAMILIES

Workers' families (including those who are non-EC nationals) also enjoy rights to free movement.

- Family members generally include spouse plus both dependent ascendants and descendants (but see *Netherlands v Reed*)

- Rights of exit, entry and residence for families are contained in secondary legislation and are largely as for workers themselves

- Family members may take up employment and enjoy education (cf academic and vocational) and social advantage as for domestic workers' dependants (see, also, Art 12)

OTHER RIGHTS INCLUDE:

- To be treated equally with domestic workers with regard to work issues and social advantages, etc (linguistic exceptions may exist)

- To remain after retirement due to age or ill health (Art 39 and Reg 1251/70/EEC)

- Right to install family members in host State

THE 'PUBLIC SERVICE' exception to the equality rules:

- Art 39(4) provides that the rights may be denied to migrant workers wishing to work in the public service

- Once more, ECJ has interpreted restrictions narrowly, e.g. *Re Public Employees*

- Commission has taken similar approach – see Notice 1988 (OJ 72/2)

WORKERS' Rights in Relation to FREE MOVEMENT

Under the doctrine of direct effect (Chapters 5 and 6), individuals may normally enforce their Community law rights before national courts. The ECJ has been particularly concerned to emphasise that Art 39 EC provides rights to individuals and in Case 167/73, *Commission v France*, the *French Seamen* case, held that Art 39 is 'directly applicable in the legal system of every Member State'. In addition, it was provided that all conflicting national law should be immediately rendered inapplicable.

Furthermore, the Court has also made it clear that the Treaty Article not only places obligations on Member States to ensure the facilitation of free movement, but also places a duty on individuals to do likewise. In *Bosman*, for example, the defendants in the action were, amongst others, the Belgium Football Association, while in Case C-282/98, *Roman Angonese v Cassa di Risparmio di Bolzana Spa* (the *Angonese* case), the ECJ specifically explained that the Community law principle of free movement of workers, places obligations not only to public bodies but also on private persons. This means that the rules are horizontally directly effectice.

In addition, should a Member State fail to comply with its obligations in relation to the free movement, the Commission (or second Member State) may initiate enforcement proceedings against that State (Arts 226, 227 and 228 EC, also discussed in Chapter 6).

i. Freedom of establishment and freedom to provide services

In addition to promoting the free movement of workers and their families within the Community, the Treaty also provides similar rights to the self-employed, businesses and those wishing to provide a service in another Member State.

Articles 43–48 EC prohibit restrictions from being placed on those who wish to establish a business in a host State, while Arts 49–55 EC afford the right of free movement to those who wish to provide a service in a host State, without setting up a permanent base in that State.

While the Treaty provides three sets of provisions covering the free movement of the three different groups of economically active persons, the Court has emphasised that much common ground that exists between them. In Case 48/75, *Royer*, for example, the Court observed that the free movement of workers, freedom of establishment and freedom to provide services are all *'based on the same principles in so far as they concern the entry into and the residence in the territory of Member States of persons covered by Community law and the prohibition of all discrimination between them on grounds of nationality'*.

It should be borne in mind, however, that while the various provisions have much in common – with regard to natural legal persons, at least – the rules applying to artificial legal persons can be quite different.

VII. RIGHTS OF ESTABLISHMENT (ARTS 43–48 EC)

Article 43 EC provides EU citizens with the right to establish a business (that is, set up a permanent base) in a host State under the same conditions as those enjoyed by nationals of that State.

This right is also applicable to the setting up of agencies, branches or subsidiaries of companies or firms that have already been established in another State. (Article 48 EC specifically provides that such businesses must be treated in the same way as natural persons.)

Those carrying out the activities set out above are required to comply with the national laws applicable in the host State unless those laws can be shown to discriminate on the basis of nationality. Such discrimination is prohibited both by Art 43 EC and, in a more general manner, by Art 12 EC. Discriminatory rules will be seen as conflicting with Community law and must consequently be set aside.

Just as Art 39 EC provides the framework for the free movement of workers, so Art 43 EC provides a framework for rights of establishment. Once more, the relevant primary legislation is supported and expanded upon by secondary legislation and decisions of the ECJ.

1. What amounts to 'establishment'?

The ECJ has defined establishment as 'the actual pursuit of an economic activity through a fixed establishment in another Member State for an indefinite period' (Case C-221/89, *Factortame*).

i. Natural legal persons

In some situations there maybe some initial confusion over whether someone is employed or self-employed. The Court, however, has made it clear that anyone who is working under the control of another and is receiving a wage or salary will be considered a worker, while those involved in the running of a business will be considered to be self-employed. (Case C-456/02 *Trojani v Centre public d'aide sociale*.)

ii. Artificial legal persons

As touched on above, in addition to natural legal persons, who wish to establish themselves in a host State, artificial legal persons are also afforded rights of establishment. (Art 48 EC should be read here, as it provides a list of artificial persons who may benefit from rules on establishment.)

To enjoy such rights, companies must demonstrate that they are already legally established in one Member State, often known as the 'primary State', and wish to conduct business in a second Member State, or 'secondary State' (Art 48 EC).

This has, on occasional, been problematic, as companies registered in one State and established in a second State, have then moved their main place of business to the second State, in order to benefit from a more lax regulatory regimes (as in Case 81/87, *R v HM Treasury ex parte Daily Mail*, where the business was able to avoid onerous taxation rules in its 'home' State). The ECJ have since provided that only the primary State can raise objections to such behaviour (Case C-212/97, *Centros*).

2. Rights of the self-employed and their families: exit, entry and residence

Art 7 of Directive 2004/38 is quite specific in that it provides rights not only for workers and their families but also self-employed persons and their families. Consequently, the rights outlined above, in relation to exit, entry and residence, will apply in the same manner to the self-employed and their families, as they do to workers and their families and so therefore need not be reiterated here.

As the ECJ has also provided that the rules relating to workers and the self-employed are based on the same principles (*Royer*), it can safely be assumed that an analogous approach should be taken in regard to their interpretation and application.

3. Equality: what amounts to 'discrimination'?

In line with its case law in the area of free movement workers – and free movement of goods – the Court has provided that both directly and indirectly discriminatory rules may breach Art 43 EC.

While national rules which apply to non-nationals only will be prima facie discriminatory, national laws which appear to apply equally to non-nationals and nationals alike, may also breach Art 43 EC (Case 71/76, *Thieffry*). In Case 143/87, *Stanton v INASTI*, the Court went even further by providing that any national rule, whether discriminatory or not, which 'might place Community citizens at a disadvantage' will be prohibited *unless* it can be objectively justified by the State wishing to apply it.

The question of whether 'reverse discrimination' is prohibited by Art 43 EC has also been considered by the ECJ. Reverse discrimination occurs when the discrimination complained of takes place within the national's home State. An illustration of the problem can be found in Case 115/78, *Knoors v Secretary of State for Economic Affairs*, where qualifications obtained by *Mr Knoors*, a Dutch national, while resident in Belgium were not recognised by the Dutch State when he returned home to Holland.

It is now clear that any rule which discourages free movement of goods, persons or services is likely to come within the prohibitions of Community law – unless it is indirect discrimination, which may be objectively justified. (The issue of 'justification' is set out above under the heading of 'The public interest justification', which lists the conditions which must be fulfilled if a rule is not to fall foul of Community law, as provided by the Court in the case of *Gebhard*.)

i. Recognition of qualifications

National rules relating to qualifications can result in a significant barrier to the free movement of persons. An example of this can be found with regard to solicitors in England and Wales, whose qualifications must comply with rules set by the Law Society. Failure to comply with such rules will result in an individual being prohibited from carrying out his/her profession.

Under Art 47 EC, the Council is provided with the authority to issue directives in regard to recognition of training and qualifications obtained within the Community and, as a result, a considerable amount of harmonising legislation has been enacted. (Directives 77/249/EEC and 98/5/EC, for example, relate specifically to legal qualifications). However not all professions are covered in this way and in the absence of such legislation, the ECJ has held that national authorities have an obligation to consider the training and/or qualifications held by a non-national and compare them to the domestic provision/requirements. Where they are found to be equivalent, the host State must recognise them as such (Case 340/89, *Vlassopoulou*).

If they are found not to be equivalent, the host State must provide reasons for its decision, which must be open to judicial review (Case 222/86, *UNECTEF v Heylens*). If qualifications are found to be 'part equivalent', a host State may require further training to be undertaken in order to 'make up the difference'.

ii. Limitations on freedom of establishment

As we have already seen in relation to workers, restrictive and/or discriminatory measures may be justified on grounds of public policy, security and health and also with regard to employment in the public sector. Similar grounds may also be argued in relation to establishment (and the provision of services).

iii Limitation on grounds of 'public policy, public service and public health'

Art 46 EC provides for limitation of rights 'on grounds of public policy, public security or public health'. The Court has held that these grounds should be applied in a similar manner to those found under Art 39(3) EC (Case 36/74, *Walrave and Koch*) and, indeed, the secondary legislation expanding upon this derogation specifically relates to both workers and establishment (Directive 2004/38).

iv. The exercise of 'official authority' limitation

Article 45 EC provides that rules concerning establishment may not apply to those who 'exercise official authority'.

The exception will be relevant in relation to the exercise of an official (State) power. The ECJ has confirmed that it is to be applied in a similar manner to the exception found under Art 39(4) EC, that is, the 'employment in the public service' exception to free movement of workers (Case 2/74, *Reyners v Belgium*). As the Court has interpreted the 'public service' exception narrowly with regard to Art 39 EC (see above), a similar approach can safely be assumed here.

4. Enforcing rights of establishment

Case 2/74, *Reyners*, provides authority that Art 43 EC is directly effective.

In Case 36/74, *Walrave and Koch*, which related to the rights of the self-employed, the Court appeared to extend the scope of the legislation beyond merely the actions of public authorities. In view of the decisions of the Court in *Bosman* and *Angonese* (discussed above) and the analogous approach of the Court in all areas relating to free movement, it is likely that

Art 43 EC is at least partly horizontally directly effective, although there has yet to be a totally decisive judgement.

VIII. FREEDOM OF MOVEMENT TO PROVIDE SERVICES (ARTS 49–55 EC)

While rights of establishment relate to rights enjoyed by EU citizens who wish to set up of a permanent base in a host State (for an unspecified period), rights of free movement to provide services normally relate to the carrying out of an economic activity for a *temporary* period, where the provider has no permanent base in that State.

The distinction may be difficult to draw on occasion – for example, in *Gebhard*, it was ruled that a service provider may have an office or other base in the host State from which he provides his (temporary) service(s). However, in that case the ECJ also provided that '*the temporary nature of the activities in question has to be determined in the light, not only of the duration of the provision of the service, but also of its regularity, periodicity or continuity.*'

Art 49 EC has also been held to prohibit measures that restrict the provision of services, where the *recipient* moves to a host State to obtain the service (Joined Cases 286/82 and 26/83, *Luisi* and *Carbone*, and Case 186/87, *Cowan v Tresor Public*). It also appears to cover situations where the service moves but neither provider nor recipient move (e.g. internet provided services), *or* where both parties move to a third State – what is important is that there is an inter-State element to the transaction.

1. What is a 'service'?

Art 50 EC provides that to be considered a 'service', the service must be 'provided for remuneration' (which has been supported by the ECJ in Case 52/79, *Debauve*, where the Court made it clear that services provided gratuitously are not included). The Article also provides examples, such as activities of an industrial or commercial nature, of craftsmen and of the professions.

The ECJ has interpreted 'services' widely to include medical services, vocational training and tourism, and is likely to include any (lawful) temporary presence in a host State, unless specifically covered by another area of the Treaty.

2. Rights of service providers

i. Rights of exit and entry

Rights include the right to exit a home State and enter a host State in very much the same way as provided to workers and the self-employed, as discussed above. However, as those wishing to provide – or receive – a service do not wish to establish a permanent base in a host State, rights *do not* include residence rights for either the provider or receiver of a service, or his/her family.

ii. Protection from discrimination

Art 49 EC requires the elimination of all discrimination based on nationality, against non-national providers (or receivers) of services. This Article is supported by the more general Art 12 EC, which requires the elimination of discrimination based on nationality.

Once more, the elimination of such discrimination has been extended to national measures which impede free movement, without necessarily directly discriminating (Case C-384/93, *Alpine Investments*). Again, where the national rule is not directly discriminatory, it may be objectively justifiable (in Cases C-369 and C-376/96, *Arblade*, the principles developed in *Gebhard* – discussed above – were once more applied).

3. Exceptions to the right of free movement to provide services

Members States may, once more, derogate from their obligations to provide rights of free movement of services on similar grounds to those already considered in terms of workers and establishment.

i. What does the Treaty say?

Public policy, public security or public health

Art 55 EC specifically provides that the derogations, relating to establishment, found in Art 46 EC will also apply to the right to move freely to provide a service. Consequently, discussion provided above in relation to such derogations will be relevant to consider in relation to services.

Exercise of official authority

Art 55 also provides that the derogation relating to the exercise of official authority found in Art 45, will apply in the same manner to services.

4. Interpretation of the exceptions to free movement of services by the ECJ

As has already been discussed, in regard to workers and establishment, exceptions to the right of free movement have been interpreted restrictively by the Court, thus ensuring that restrictions on free movement are kept to a minimum. Unsurprisingly, as all 'four freedoms' are intended to support the creation of a single market, the Court's approach here mirrors its approach in relation to free movement of workers and rights of establishment – and also to a certain extent, free movement of goods (discussed in Chapter 7).

5. Enforcing rights to provide and receive services

Case 33/74, *Van Binsbergen*, provides authority that Art 49 EC has direct effect.

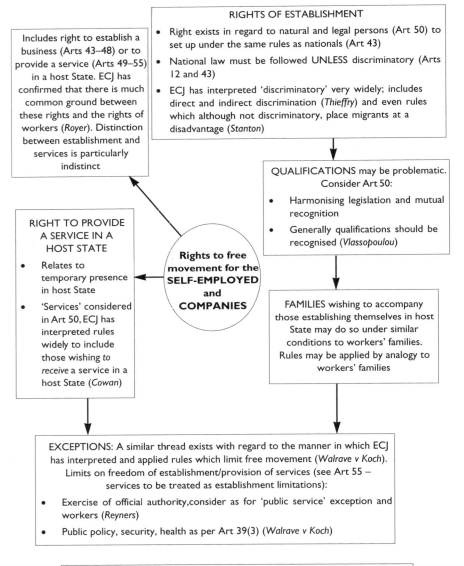

RIGHTS OF ESTABLISHMENT

- Right exists in regard to natural and legal persons (Art 50) to set up under the same rules as nationals (Art 43)
- National law must be followed UNLESS discriminatory (Arts 12 and 43)
- ECJ has interpreted 'discriminatory' very widely; includes direct and indirect discrimination (*Thieffry*) and even rules which although not discriminatory, place migrants at a disadvantage (*Stanton*)

Includes right to establish a business (Arts 43–48) or to provide a service (Arts 49–55) in a host State. ECJ has confirmed that there is much common ground between these rights and the rights of workers (*Royer*). Distinction between establishment and services is particularly indistinct

QUALIFICATIONS may be problematic. Consider Art 50:

- Harmonising legislation and mutual recognition
- Generally qualifications should be recognised (*Vlassopoulou*)

RIGHT TO PROVIDE A SERVICE IN A HOST STATE

- Relates to temporary presence in host State
- 'Services' considered in Art 50, ECJ has interpreted rules widely to include those wishing *to receive* a service in a host State (*Cowan*)

Rights to free movement for the SELF-EMPLOYED and COMPANIES

FAMILIES wishing to accompany those establishing themselves in host State may do so under similar conditions to workers' families. Rules may be applied by analogy to workers' families

EXCEPTIONS: A similar thread exists with regard to the manner in which ECJ has interpreted and applied rules which limit free movement (*Walrave v Koch*). Limits on freedom of establishment/provision of services (see Art 55 – services to be treated as establishment limitations):

- Exercise of official authority, consider as for 'public service' exception and workers (*Reyners*)
- Public policy, security, health as per Art 39(3) (*Walrave v Koch*)

FREE MOVEMENT in Relation to ESTABLISHMENT and the PROVISION of SERVICES

9 Competition Law

As has already been considered, the primary aim of the Community is the creation of a common market. This has meant that the Community has had to ensure that all unnecessary barriers to trade are removed. Member States have to play their part by, for example, ensuring the removal of all customs duties while also ensuring that national laws do not, amongst other things, create unnecessary pecuniary or quantitative restrictions to trade or hinder the free movement of persons within the Community.

While these activities contribute to the aim of integrating the economies of Member States, they would not, alone, be sufficient to ensure the creation of a single market within Europe. The Treaty recognises that 'undertakings' (businesses of various types, from single traders to multinational corporations) also have their part to play in ensuring the creation of a common market.

Article 3(g) of the EC Treaty provides that one of the activities of the Community is to ensure that 'competition in the internal market is not distorted'. The Community consequently provides undertakings with specific obligations relating to competition by virtue of Arts 81 and 82 EC. These Articles prohibit undertakings from entering into anti-competitive agreements or from abusing a dominant market position respectively.

I. THE AIMS OF COMMUNITY COMPETITION LAW

The aims of EC competition law are broad, complementing those of free movement. While rules relating to free movement remove barriers to trade set up by Member States, EC competition law attempts to control the barriers to trade that may be set up by commercial undertakings. The primary aim of competition law can consequently be defined as aiding economic integration within the Community. The rules relating to competition also, however, fulfil other functions, including the following:

- consumer protection – rules on competition discourage price fixing, excessive charges, and so on and encourage low prices, high quality and greater choice;

- efficiency – efficiency (e.g. the most effective use of raw materials) often suffers in a monopoly situation, but is normally encouraged by competition;

- fairness – the Preamble to the EC Treaty refers to 'fair competition' and this can be seen to relate to areas such as the prohibition of government subsidies, and so on creating a healthy market/level playing field, where small and medium size enterprises, as well as large firms, may prosper.

1. The basis of EC competition rules

The rules contained in Arts 81 and 82 EC follow those established by the United States's Sherman Act, 1890. This Act prohibits 'every contract, combination or conspiracy in restraint of trade' and 'the monopolisation of trade and commerce' and has been adopted in a number of other countries, such as Canada, Ireland, Italy and Sweden. The Act, in effect, prohibits distortion of free competition resulting from collusion or other conduct

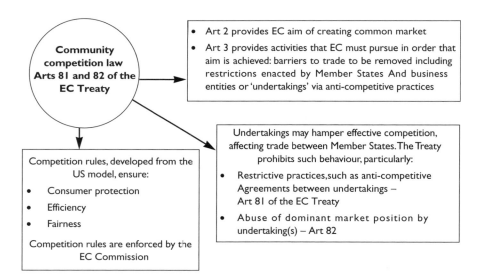

between two or more undertakings and also from the abuse of predominant market power by one.

II. THE PROHIBITION OF RESTRICTIVE PRACTICES (ART 81 EC)

1. Overview

Article 81 EC, in effect, prohibits undertakings from entering into anti-competitive agreements that may have a restrictive effect on inter-Community trade. The Article requires that such agreements be declared void, unless there is a sufficiently valid reason to allow them to receive an exemption.

2. What does the Treaty say?

Article 81(1) EC prohibits 'all agreements between undertakings, decisions by associations of undertakings and concerted practices which may affect trade between Member States and which have as their object or effect the prevention, restriction or distortion of competition within the common market'. It then goes on to provide examples of the types of agreement that are prohibited.

In order to develop an understanding of the provisions contained within Art 81 EC, it is helpful to break the Article down into its constituent parts, namely:

- whose agreements are prohibited;
- types of agreement which are prohibited;
- the aims and/or effects of such agreements;
- the possible exemption of beneficial agreements.

As would be expected, Art 81 EC has been the subject of extensive interpretation by the ECJ.

i. 'Undertakings'

The term 'undertaking' has been interpreted widely to include every type of entity from a single individual to a multinational corporation, provided they are capable of becoming engaged in economic activity (Case 41/90, *Hofner and Elsner v Macrotron*). It is not necessary that the undertaking have legal personality. The width of the term 'undertaking' can be demonstrated by Commission Decision 78/516/EEC, Re *Unitel*, where it was provided that an opera singer was an undertaking for the purpose of competition rules.

The term has also been held to include parent companies established outside the EC. Such companies will be held responsible for acts of their subsidiaries within the EC (Case 48/69, *ICI v Commission*, the *Dyestuff* case, and Cases C-89, etc/85, *Ahlström oy v Commission*, the *Woodpulp* case).

ii. 'Associations of undertakings'

This term has been held to incorporate trade associations and includes non-binding recommendations as well as decisions of such associations.

iii. 'Agreements'

The term 'agreements' has also been interpreted widely and inclusively. It has been held to include both formal and informal agreements, for example, a gentleman's agreement (Cases 41, 44 and 45/69, *ACF Chemiefarma v Commission*, the *Quinine Cartel* case) and unilateral contracts (Case 107/82R, *AEG-Telefunken v Commission*, where AEG refused to admit dealers to its dealership network). Agreements which are vertical (between producers and distributors) as well as horizontal (between, for example, producers) may be caught by Art 81 EC (Cases 56 and 58/64, *Consten and Grundig*).

In Case 193/83, *Windsurfing v Commission*, the Court explained that it is necessary to look at the whole agreement and it was held to be irrelevant that certain restrictions within the agreement did not affect trade.

iv. 'Concerted practices'

Concerted practices were defined in the *Dyestuff* case as 'a form of co-ordination between undertakings which, without having reached the stage where an agreement properly so called has been concluded, knowingly substitutes practical co-operation between them for the risks of competition'.

No contract need exist, and the practice is more a type of behaviour than an agreement. In *Dyestuff*, it was accepted that what may appear to be price fixing at first sight can sometimes be 'oligopolistic interdependence' (i.e. responding to movements in the market – such as oil companies responding to changes in competitors' prices – with no actual collusion). The burden of proof is, however, on the defendant to demonstrate that there has been no collusion.

As can be seen, the Court has provided a broad view of the nature of 'agreement' under Art 81 EC, as to do otherwise would leave a loophole through which less formal agreements could slip, leading to the distortion of competition within the Community. This attitude can be summed up by the Court's dicta in Joined Cases C-2/01 & C-3/01 P, *BAI & Commission v Bayer*, in which the Court said that the concept of an agreement under Art 81(1) *'centres around the existence of a concurrence of wills between at least two parties'* ... with *'the form in which it is manifested being unimportant.'*

Once it has been established that an agreement exists, it is then necessary to consider whether the agreement is one that is prohibited by Art 81.

3. 'Which may affect trade between Member States'

i. The need for there to be a potential impact on 'inter-Community' trade

In situations where the impact is limited to only one Member State, national law will apply and the Community will have no jurisdiction to act (Case 61/80, *Co-operative Stremsel en Kleurselfabriek* and the *Woodpulp* case).

ii. The nature of the impact on trade

The Court has held that there is no need to prove actual effect – the mere potential for such an outcome is sufficient for an agreement to fall within Art 81.

A 'test' for behaviour amounting to such market distortion was developed by the ECJ in Case 56/65, *Société Technique Minière v Maschinenbau (STM)*, where it explained that: *'It must be possible to foresee ... that the agreement in question may have an influence, direct or indirect, actual or potential, on the pattern of trade between Member States.'*

The Court has also held that it does not matter that the impact – potential or otherwise – is not detrimental; indeed, in the *Consten and Grundig* case, the effect of the agreement was an increase in trade, but the agreement was still held to come within the scope of the competition rules.

iii. The 'object or effect' of the agreement

The Court has held that the 'object' of the agreement and the 'effect' of the agreement should be considered separately (*Consten and Grundig*).

- Agreements whose object is anti-competitive – If the 'object' is found to be anti-competitive, it will be unnecessary to consider the 'effect', as the agreement will automatically come within the scope of Art 81 EC.

- Agreements whose object is *not* anti-competitive – Where the object of the agreement is *not* anti-competitive, the impact of the agreement – potential or otherwise – will have to be considered.

The Treaty only prohibits agreements that prevent, restrict or distort competition within the common market. Article 81(1) EC provides examples of such effects, namely agreements which:

- involve price fixing or enforce other trading conditions;

- limit or control production, markets, technical development or investment;

- share markets or sources of supply;

- place parties at a disadvantage by applying dissimilar conditions to equivalent transactions; or

- require supplementary contracts to be concluded, as a term of the original agreement, where such a supplementary contract has no connection to the original agreement.

The 'Rule of Reason' approach

A 'Rule of Reason' approach is commonly used in the United States. Under this approach, the reason for the agreement is considered and, if it is not anti-competitive, the agreement may be removed from the scope of prohibitive legislation. There has been much debate as to how relevant the rule is in relation to the Community's competition laws as, despite the best of motives, there may still be a restrictive effect on trade (e.g. *Consten and Grundig* and Case 258/78, *Nungesser*). It would however seem largely irrelevant due to the possibility of a prohibited agreement being 'exempted' under Art 81(3), should its positive impact outweigh its anti-competitive impact. (Art 81(3) is discussed below.)

The extent of the effect: the de minimis rule

There must be a possibility of an appreciable amount of inter-Community trade being affected, as Art 81(1) EC is subject to a *de minimis* rule. This can be explained by consideration of Case 5/69, *Volk v Vervaecke*. Volk had entered into an agreement that involved an exclusive distribution deal but, as Volk produced less than 1 per cent of washing machines within the relevant market, there was no possibility of the agreement having an appreciable – or sufficient – effect on trade.

The Commission has issued assistance on what is appreciable in their Guidance on the Effect on Trade (OJ 2004 C 101/81) in which they developed a 'test' (known as the NAAT test). Under this test the undertakings aggregate market share (over 5 per cent) and turnover (over 40 million euros) will be definitive.

4. The consequences of infringing Art 81(1) EC: (Art 81(2) EC)

If an agreement is found to come within the scope of Art 81(1) EC, Art 81(2) provides that the agreement 'shall be automatically void'.

However, it should be noted that where only *part* of an agreement falls within the scope of Art 81(1) EC, it may be possible for the offending terms to be severed while leaving the rest of the agreement intact. (In the United Kingdom, this is commonly known as the 'blue pencil' test in relation to contract terms). In addition certain apparently prohibited agreements may be 'excepted' under Art 81(3) EC, which is discussed below.

5. Exemptions to Art 81(2): Art 81(3) EC

As already seen, certain agreements do not come within the scope of Art 81 as their effect is considered insignificant (the *di minimus* rule, above). In addition, the Treaty, under Art 81(3) EC, provides that certain agreements, although restrictive and within the scope of Art 81(1), may nevertheless gain an exemption. Such an exemption will result in Art 81(2) being inapplicable.

The reason for such exemptions is that the Community recognises that certain agreements may have positive effects that outweigh any possible detrimental effect on trade (in rather the same manner as quantitative restrictions on trade may be 'saved' under Art 30 EC). The Treaty lays down four conditions that must, however, be satisfied before an exemption can be granted. The agreement must:

- improve the production or distribution of goods, or promote technical or economic progress; and

- allow consumers (that is, members of the public and other undertakings) to enjoy a fair share of the resulting benefit; while

- not imposing restrictions on the undertakings which are unnecessary to the above objectives; providing

- it does not allow the undertakings the possibility of eliminating competition in respect of a substantial part of the products in question (usually agreements between undertakings with a large market share are considered as eliminating competition).

6. Enforcement of Art 81 EC: Regulation 1/2003 EC

Enforcement of Competition law in the Community is now shared between the Commission, national competition authorities and national courts. In addition, an European Competition Network has been set up to allow for co-ordination and co-operation between national authorities.

Before the introduction of Regulation 1/2003, it was possible for undertakings to submit a request to the Commission for an exemption from the prohibitive effects of Art 81(1). If successful, the Commission would either issue a 'comfort letter', informally indicating that an agreement was likely to be outside the scope of Art 81, or an 'individual exemption' confirming that the agreement fell within the scope of Art 81(1) EC, but was exempted under Art 81(3).

Such measures are no longer available under the new enforcement regime and it is consequently up to the undertakings themselves to assess whether their agreement breaches Community rules. In order to assist undertakings, the Commission has, however, issued Guidelines on the application of Art 81(3). If an agreement is found to be prohibited by Art 81(1), the undertakings will be required to cease their anti-competitive behaviour and may also be subject to a fine.

In addition, Art 81 has direct effect (Case 127/73, *BRT v SABAM* & Regulation 1/2003), which allows for parties who have suffered harm as a result of an anti-competitive agreement to bring a claim for damages in a national court. (Where a competition case before a national court involves the question of the application of Community competition rules, the court

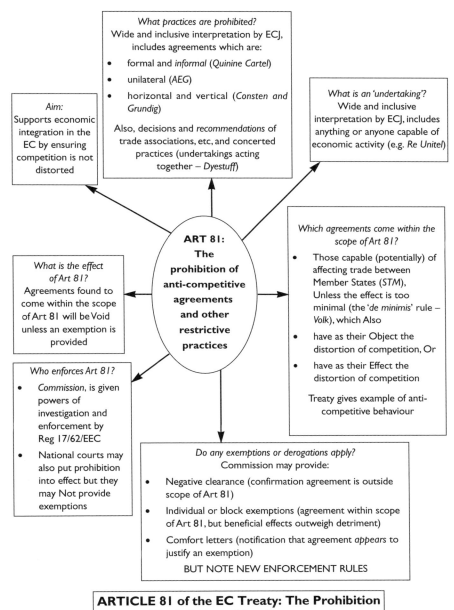

What practices are prohibited?
Wide and inclusive interpretation by ECJ, includes agreements which are:

- formal and *informal* (*Quinine Cartel*)
- unilateral (*AEG*)
- horizontal and vertical (*Consten and Grundig*)

Also, decisions and *recommendations* of trade associations, etc, and concerted practices (undertakings acting together – *Dyestuff*)

What is an 'undertaking'?
Wide and inclusive interpretation by ECJ, includes anything or anyone capable of economic activity (e.g. *Re Unitel*)

Aim:
Supports economic integration in the EC by ensuring competition is not distorted

ART 81:
The prohibition of anti-competitive agreements and other restrictive practices

Which agreements come within the scope of Art 81?

- Those capable (potentially) of affecting trade between Member States (*STM*), Unless the effect is too minimal (the '*de minimis*' rule – *Volk*), which Also
- have as their Object the distortion of competition, Or
- have as their Effect the distortion of competition

Treaty gives example of anti-competitive behaviour

What is the effect of Art 81?
Agreements found to come within the scope of Art 81 will be Void unless an exemption is provided

Who enforces Art 81?

- *Commission*, is given powers of investigation and enforcement by Reg 17/62/EEC
- National courts may also put prohibition into effect but they may Not provide exemptions

Do any exemptions or derogations apply?
Commission may provide:

- Negative clearance (confirmation agreement is outside scope of Art 81)
- Individual or block exemptions (agreement within scope of Art 81, but beneficial effects outweigh detriment)
- Comfort letters (notification that agreement *appears* to justify an exemption)

BUT NOTE NEW ENFORCEMENT RULES

ARTICLE 81 of the EC Treaty: The Prohibition of Anti-Competitive Agreements

may, of course, make use of the preliminary reference procedure under Art 234 EC (see Chapter 6))

III. ABUSE OF A DOMINANT MARKET POSITION (ART 82 EC)

Article 82, like Art 81, seeks to prevent undertakings from becoming involved in anti-competitive behaviour. It does this by prohibiting abuse of a dominant market position within the Community. The Article goes on to provide examples of abusive behaviour. It should be understood at the outset that the Article does not prohibit dominance, merely the abuse of dominance position within the EU Art 82 EC provides:

> Any abuse by one or more undertakings of a dominant position within the common market or in a substantial part of it shall be prohibited as incompatible with the common market in so far as it may affect trade between Member States. Once more, consideration of decisions of the ECJ is important to gaining an understanding of the extent and effect of the Treaty Article.

1. 'One or more undertakings'

Article 82 EC refers to 'abuse by one or more undertakings' of a dominant position. The term 'undertaking' has been interpreted in the same inclusive manner as for Art 81.

There has, however, been some argument as to whether collective or joint dominance should come within the scope of Art 81 or Art 82. While unilateral behaviour obviously comes within the scope of Art 82, the situation where two or more undertakings operate in a parallel manner is far less clear.

The ECJ appears to have rejected the possibility of oligopolies jointly enjoying a dominant position (Case 85/76, *Hoffman-La Roche v Commission*), suggesting that Art 81 EC more fittingly catches such agreements.

The Commission's view apparently differs, as can be evidenced in Cases T-68 and 77–78/89, Re *Italian Flat Glass*, where the Commission concluded that three glass producers held a collective dominant position in the flat glass market. Academics have, however, argued that Art 82 EC will only need to apply where the behaviour of the undertakings is outside the scope of Art 81.

2. 'Dominant position'

While dominance itself is *not* prohibited, an undertaking must be shown to be dominant in a particular market before there can be any question of 'abuse'. It is therefore necessary to consider the following issues:

- the exact nature of the 'relevant market';
- the undertaking's 'dominance' of that market.

i. The 'relevant' market

Dominance can exist in both the supply and purchase of goods or services. The relevant market needs to be isolated before dominance can be assessed. This may be done by considering issues such as the availability of identical or interchangeable goods or services, the relevant territory or geographical influences and also temporal changes. Each needs to be considered in turn.

Isolating the relevant product or service

Consideration will need to be given to the product or service supplied or produced, including any products that are identical, equivalent, interchangeable or 'substitutable' with those in question.

The leading case in this area is Case 27/76, *United Brands v Commission*. In *United Brands*, involving a major supplier of bananas in Europe, the Commission concluded that the relevant product market (RPM) was bananas. The undertaking argued, however, that the RPM was fruit, as a rise in banana prices would result in a switch by consumers to other fruit (in economic terms, the cross-elasticity of demand). The ECJ concluded that the RPM was bananas, as a significant proportion of banana consumers were unable to switch to hard fruit (particularly the elderly, very young, infirm and, of course, the toothless!).

A further illustrative case on how the relevant market may be isolated is Case 6/72, *Europemballage and Continental Can v Commission* (*Continental Can*). Here it was argued that the undertaking held a dominant position with regard to the supply of metal containers for meat and fish products. While the Commission considered the extent to which consumers could switch to glass or plastic containers, the ECJ concluded that it was also necessary to consider how easily the manufacturers and suppliers of metal containers for vegetables could adapt their production processes to compete with Continental Can products (the cross-elasticity of supply). It can therefore be concluded that when considering the extent of the RPM, 'interchangeability' is particularly important, both with regards to the supply of alternatives and consumer demand for such alternatives.

The relevant geographical market (RGM)

Article 82 EC does not require that dominance be proven throughout the Community, but it must be shown that it occurs in a 'substantial part of it'. The territories of individual Member States have been found to be a 'substantial part' of the EC (e.g. Ireland in Cases C-241 and 242/91P, *RTE* and *ITP v Commission*).

The RGM of a product may be affected by such issues as the cost of transport and consumer taste and these issues should be taken into account when determining the RGM. Where goods are easily and relatively cheaply transportable, the RGM may be considered to be the whole of the Community.

The relevant seasonal or temporal market

It should also be noted that it may, on occasion, also be relevant to consider the temporal market. In *United Brands*, for example, it was argued that the Commission should have considered that in summer, bananas enjoy increased competition from soft, 'summer' fruits.

Additional guidance on defining the RPM and RGM can be found in the Commission Notice on the Defining of the Relevant Market for the Purposes of Community Competition Law (1997) OJ C372. While it is the Court which provides the definitive interpretation of such issues, the Commission's input is relevant, as it is the Commission that enforces competition rules on behalf of the Community.

ii. Dominance

Having ascertained the RPM, it is necessary to then consider whether or not a particular undertaking is dominant in that market. It is consequently essential to consider what type of behaviour may indicate that an undertaking is dominant. 'Dominance' has been defined by the ECJ as 'a position of economic strength enjoyed by an undertaking which enables it to prevent competition being maintained in the relevant market by giving it the power to behave to an appreciable extent independently of its competitors, customers and ultimately of its consumers' (*United Brands*).

This definition was extended in Case 5/85, *AKZO v Commission*, where the Court provided that dominance could also be evidenced by 'the power to exclude competition...may also involve the ability to eliminate or seriously weaken existing competition or to prevent potential competitors from entering the market'. Such decisions indicate that dominance involves an undertaking being sufficiently powerful so as to be able to act with little thought as to how its competitors, potential competitors or consumers may react to its actions. A number of factors may bring about this situation, including the size of an undertaking's market share, the structure of the particular market and also obstacles to entering the market. Each will be considered in turn.

The relevance of market share in assessing dominance

The greater the size of an undertaking's market share, the greater the likelihood of dominance. While few undertakings will achieve 100 per cent share of the market, an undertaking with over 50 per cent market share would appear to be dominant.

The relevance of market structure

Where market share is relatively low, it will be necessary to carry out a market analysis, involving consideration of the market structure. In *United Brands*, for example, market share was calculated to be between 40 and 45 per cent. In addition to United Brands' market share, the market share of its nearest competitors was also considered. This was found to be 16 per cent and, by comparison, United Brands was consequently considered to be dominant.

Obstacles to entering the market

Even if an undertaking enjoys a relatively high market share, this need not always denote dominance. If it is relatively easy for competitors to enter the relevant market, the necessary autocracy is absent. The easier it is to enter the relevant market, the more competitive the market can be seen to be.

Barriers to entry may include high investment costs, difficulty in obtaining raw materials or supplies, technical knowledge and distribution difficulties and where such problems are significant, the market is likely to be dominated by existing participants.

3. 'Abuse'

In order for Art 82 EC to apply, 'abuse' must be demonstrated. In Case 322/81, *Michelin v Commission*, the Court held that a firm in a dominant position has a 'special responsibility' not to allow its conduct to impair competition. 'Abuse' is an objective concept, and there is no need for the undertaking to have intended harm in order for particular behaviour to be considered abusive (*Hoffman-La Roche*). The Treaty provides a non-inclusive list of abusive behaviour and, as the *United Brands* case provides an example of most of the abuses on the list, the case is essential reading. Other relevant cases include:

- imposing unfair prices – *Hoffman-La Roche* (granting of 'loyalty' discounts);
- predatory pricing – *AKZO* (part of a strategy to eliminate competition);
- refusing to supply – Cases 6 and 7/73, *Commercial Solvents* (refusal to supply essential chemical to competitor);
- supplying on discriminatory terms – *Michelin* (price discounts);
- mergers/takeovers (see also merger control, below) – *Continental Can*.

4. Exemption from Art 82 EC

No exemption is available from the prohibition contained within Art 82 EC.

5. Enforcement of Art 82 EC

i. By individuals:

Art 82 EC has been held to be directly effective (Case 127/73, *BRT v SABAM*).

ii. By the Commission, national competition authorities & national courts

Regulation 1/2002 EC gives wide powers of investigation into a possible breach. The Commission – and/or national authorities – has powers to enter the undertaking's business premises, examine documents and demand that any questions it asks be answered. Where the breach is found to be either intentional or negligent, not only will the undertaking be required to desist from the anti-competitive behaviour, but a substantial fine may also be imposed.

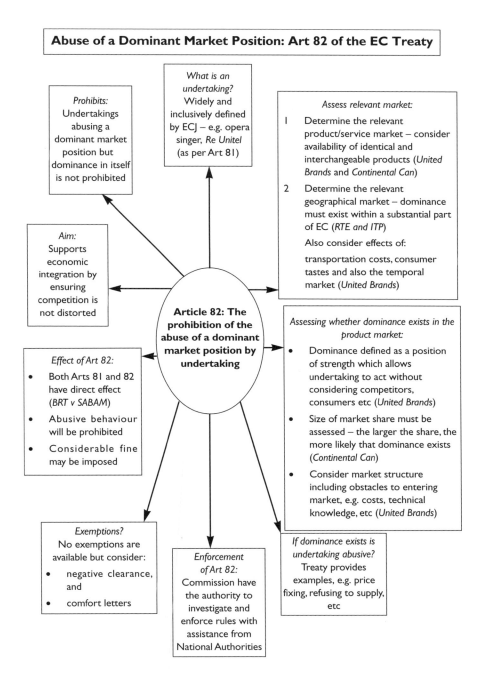

Abuse of a Dominant Market Position: Art 82 of the EC Treaty

Prohibits:
Undertakings abusing a dominant market position but dominance in itself is not prohibited

What is an undertaking?
Widely and inclusively defined by ECJ – e.g. opera singer, *Re Unitel* (as per Art 81)

Assess relevant market:

1 Determine the relevant product/service market – consider availability of identical and interchangeable products (*United Brands* and *Continental Can*)

2 Determine the relevant geographical market – dominance must exist within a substantial part of EC (*RTE and ITP*)

Also consider effects of:

transportation costs, consumer tastes and also the temporal market (*United Brands*)

Aim:
Supports economic integration by ensuring competition is not distorted

Article 82: The prohibition of the abuse of a dominant market position by undertaking

Assessing whether dominance exists in the product market:

• Dominance defined as a position of strength which allows undertaking to act without considering competitors, consumers etc (*United Brands*)

• Size of market share must be assessed – the larger the share, the more likely that dominance exists (*Continental Can*)

• Consider market structure including obstacles to entering market, e.g. costs, technical knowledge, etc (*United Brands*)

Effect of Art 82:

• Both Arts 81 and 82 have direct effect (*BRT v SABAM*)

• Abusive behaviour will be prohibited

• Considerable fine may be imposed

Exemptions?
No exemptions are available but consider:

• negative clearance, and

• comfort letters

Enforcement of Art 82:
Commission have the authority to investigate and enforce rules with assistance from National Authorities

If dominance exists is undertaking abusive?
Treaty provides examples, e.g. price fixing, refusing to supply, etc

IV. MERGER CONTROL

Mergers can have a significant effect on competition – positive as well as negative – but neither Art 81 nor Art 82 EC specifically refer to either mergers or takeovers. However, until Regulation 4064/89/EEC was adopted, these Treaty Articles were the only source of Community control.

Mergers now come under Regulation 139/2004EC, which requires that mergers and takeovers (or 'concentrations' as they are often known) which have an 'European dimension' must normally be notified to the Commission. (Such concentrations will be subject to a lower to an aggregate worldwide turnover threshold of 5000 million euros and a Community threshold of 250 million euros. Where turnover is lower than this, Member States, rather than the Commission, will investigate.) Concentrations that are not cleared by the Commission will be considered to be illegal. Factors which are taken into account by the Commission include the market share, market structure, obstacles to entry and also interests of the consumer (Commission Decision Re *Aerospatiale/Alexia/De Havilland* (Case IV/M/053) (1991) provides an example).

V. PUBLIC BODIES AND COMMUNITY COMPETITION RULES

It should be noted that both Arts 81 and 82 EC are addressed to undertakings as opposed to Member States. There is, however, nothing to prevent national authorities from becoming involved in commercial activity and, if competition rules are breached, the law will apply to a State authority in the same way as it does to other undertakings.

Government action may, in addition, reinforce anti-competitive behaviour in undertakings. Should this happen, the Community may make use of other Treaty Articles such as Art 10 EC (which places an obligation on Member States to do nothing which may jeopardise the aims of the Treaty) to circumnavigate the problem. The Treaty also provides Member States with certain obligations under Arts 86–89 EC. While outside the scope of this book, for the sake of completeness, it is necessary to be aware of the existence of these Treaty Articles.

1. Article 86 EC – State monopolies

Undertakings that enjoy 'special or exclusive rights' provided by the State would appear to be at odds with Community competition rules. Article 86 EC, however, provides a balance between 'state monopolies' (often including providers of water, gas, electricity, railways, national lotteries, etc) and Arts 81 and 82 EC by ensuring that the consequent restriction of competition is limited to that which is necessary and proportional to the aim being achieved (Case C-230/91, *Corbeau*).

2. Articles 87–89 EC – State aids

While the provision of State 'aid' (that is, subsidies, loans on favourable terms, tax write-offs and the like) to undertakings is not totally prohibited by the Treaty, aid which 'affects trade between Member States' is 'incompatible with the common market' (Art 87 EC).

Article 87 goes on to provide a list of aid which is compatible with the common market and also provides the Commission with the obligation to keep any existing State aid under review (Art 88(1) EC). New aid must also be notified to the Commission under Art 88(3) EC.

While the latter provision is directly effective, other provisions relating to State aid are not and remain largely a matter for the Commission's discretion. Any State aid that falls foul of the Treaty provisions may have to be repaid (Case 70/72, *Commission v Germany*).

Reform of State aid rules

The Commission has proposed that rules on State aid should be reformed in order to 'make state aid and policy clearer, simpler and easier to understand.' At present there is no indication as to when any new rules may be put into effect and it will consequently necessary to follow the progress of the proposed reforms on the EU's Europa web site.

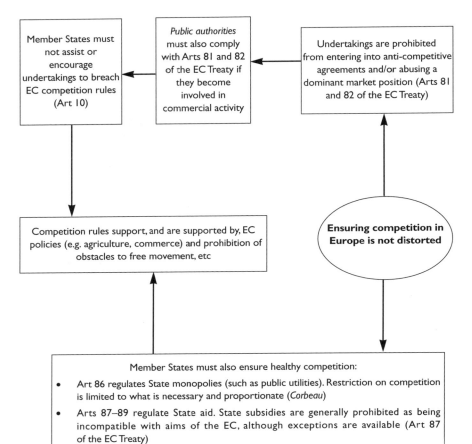

10 Revision and Examinations

This book is not intended to be a revision workbook or a guide on how to pass exams but, very briefly, some hopefully helpful tips are provided below.

I. REVISION

Before you start, ensure that you are totally familiar with the syllabus of your course. Always plan your revision well in advance, ensuring that you start early enough to complete it *and have time for relaxation*! Trying to 'learn' European law by rote is boring, hard work and unlikely to produce good results. What you need to do is ensure you understand the law and *why* it has developed as it has.

If you have worked consistently throughout your course, you should have few worries. All you will need to do is ensure that what you have learned throughout the academic year is brought to the forefront of your memory. One of the most important things to do is to discover what you do know and what areas need a little more work – there is little point in spending excessive time on areas that you are sufficiently familiar with! One of the best ways of testing your knowledge is to obtain past papers, old tutorial questions or even pick out appropriate questions from a revision workbook. Sit down and attempt to answer the questions – preferably in full and under similar constraints as will be imposed in the examination room. Check your answers against your notes or textbook and this should tell you which are your weak areas, allowing you the opportunity to concentrate your revision time on these.

As touched upon above, there is little point in sitting down with your notes or textbook and trying to learn by rote. It is far more productive to read around the areas that you are finding difficult, perhaps making your own notes and then attempt to answer further questions, once more under examination conditions.

If you make your own notes, which is always a good idea as it aids memory, make sure that they are not too detailed. If they are particularly detailed, you may find that there is little advantage in consulting them rather than a textbook, especially for last minute revision! You may also find it useful to use 'spider diagrams' or flowcharts, which can also be useful when constructing answer plans. Brain-storming is another useful way to 'encourage' your memory – don't discount it without giving it a try!

II. EXAMINATION TECHNIQUE

Success in examinations cannot be entirely put down to good (or bad) exam technique. Without an appropriate level of knowledge and understanding, it is unlikely that exam success will be enjoyed. However, good exam technique can make the difference between achieving or just missing a grade.

Exam questions will either be 'essay type' or 'problem type'. While students often profess to only being able to cope with one type or the other, there is actually very little difference in what is required and both should be approached in the same way.

First, *always* prepare an answer plan. You may feel that there is little time for such luxury in a time-constrained assessment, but in reality, you will probably save time – unplanned answers often ramble and points may be repeated or irrelevant issues discussed. Your plan need not be long or complex; often a few key words, in an appropriate order, will be sufficient.

All answers should have an introduction, a 'main' part and a conclusion. A brief – never rambling – introduction can be seen as an opportunity to 'set the scene', provide relevant background information and/or demonstrate an understanding of how the subject matter of your answer relates to the wider view of Europe. Alternatively, if you find this difficult, the introduction can be used to explain to the reader what needs to be discussed, and why, in order to answer the question.

The 'main' part of your answer should contain the 'meat'. When planning your answer, you should not only decide what you need to say, but also the order in which it is most effectively said. This will ensure that your answer flows. (I always advise students to provide a – again brief – overview of the law relevant to the question before attempting to apply/evaluate the law to the specifics of the question. This will allow students to gain marks, even if their application/evaluation is flawed!)

The exam question will require that you reach a conclusion. Never forget to do this. You may have been asked to advise someone, consider a proposition or comment on the development of law, for example. To ensure that you have actually answered the question asked, and not the one you would like to have been asked, always re-read the question before embarking on your conclusion. If you discover that you have wandered from the point or missed an important point, you will then still have the opportunity to put matters right.

Do not make any new points in your conclusion and do not be tempted to repeat arguments, although emphasising key issues is normally appropriate. It is often sufficient to say: 'In conclusion, based on the arguments (or discussion or facts) provided above, I would advise Joe that...'.

As well as planning your answers, do not forget to plan your time. Many undergraduate examinations are three hours in length; some have additional 'reading time'. Divide this time carefully between the number of questions that have to be answered and ensure that you do not spend too long on one answer to the detriment of the others. It is very important to ensure that you answer the requisite number of questions. If you are required, for example, to answer four questions, you will not attain as many marks by answering three questions particularly well as you could by answering the required four reasonably well.

I hope that it is unnecessary to remind you to check the date, time and place of the examination! Do, however, ensure that you are aware of what you may take into the examination room with you. For example, it is often possible to take in an unannotated copy of EC legislation – which you should find invaluable if you have referred to it diligently throughout your course.

All that remains now is to wish you every success! (Yes, your tutors *do* want you to do well!!)

Index